CUISINE

GRAND~MERE

CUISINE
GRAND~MERE

TRADITIONAL
FRENCH
HOME
COOKING

MARIE~PIERRE
MOINE

BARRIE & JENKINS
LONDON

Pour Mado – Madame Marcel Morange

First published in Great Britain in 1990
by Barrie & Jenkins Ltd,
Random Century House, 20 Vauxhall Bridge Road, London SW1V 2SA

British Library Cataloguing in Publication data
Moine, Marie-Pierre
  Cuisine grand-mere.
  1. Food: French dishes – Recipes
  I. Title
  641.5944

ISBN 0–7126–3630–7

Designed by David Fordham
Edited by Jo Mead and Rosamond Man
Picture research by Philippa Lewis
Line drawings by Philip Hood
Typeset by Bookworm Typesetting, Manchester
Colour separation by Scantrans, Singapore
Printed and bound in Spain by Printer Industria Gráfica, S.A. Barcelona

CONTENTS

Introduction

Some of my happiest childhood memories are of my grandparents' kitchen at Fourchettes, their house near Amboise in the Loire valley. This is troglodyte country, the land of cave dwellers, and the Fourchettes kitchen was, in fact, such a cave, separate from the house, carved out of the rocks sixty feet beneath the wood that led up to the edge of the vineyards. The cave-kitchen was a magic place. It was empty of cheerful fifties' gadgets, but full of mysteries, and large enough for us as small children to test our cycling skills around the old table when nobody was watching. It was cool in summer and mild in winter, with patches of green damp stubbornly coming up through the whitewash on the 'walls'.

I loved it for its strangeness and for the myriad good things that came from it. It was presided over by Madeleine, my grandmother's cook, who had been in the family much longer than I, and was my youngest aunt's godmother. She was the genius of the place, radiating good-humour and energy. The grown-ups, after most meals, nodded their heads contentedly and commented without fail that she was '*vraiment une bonne cuisinière, une très, très bonne cuisinière, une excellente cuisinière*'. I didn't have a great deal to compare Mado to, but, yes, her food tasted better than the food I normally ate, certainly much better than that I had at my parents' in Paris.

Like all magic places, the kitchen had its dangers. The huge black range which Mado kept constantly burning quite daunted me, a tame volcano on one side of the cave. On the other side was an ancient refrigerator so badly earthed that we children weren't allowed near it. I once disobeyed the rule and tried to open its door to steal an illicit *œuf à la neige*. It was siesta time and I was barefoot: the shock was so violent that my aunt, who tried to prize me off, got stuck too. Fortunately someone else made a dash for the mains and I live to tell the tale, wear sandals when raiding fridges, and still eat *œufs à la neige*.

The grass was greener on holiday, of course, but knowing that there was going to be a *tarte à l'oignon* or profiteroles for dinner added a glow to the afternoon. I always asked about the menu, helped pick for it in the garden and reported faithfully to the kitchen most evenings after my bath, to tail beans and stir the vinaigrette, hoping to lick a few spoons here and there, while Madeleine, eyes watering from peeling onions, fed me family gossip, solved grievances and explained why evaporated milk was better than cream in onion tart . . . Nor was I the only one listening, for the kitchen was the newsroom and general refuge of the family – Mado knew everything, wasn't partisan, dispensed sympathy, jokes and common sense. She invariably had an audience around the oiled cloth of the central table while she hovered between the big kitchen range and the chipped enamel sink. More often than not, the adults present had a glass of 'Fourchettes' wine in hand, to be concealed at once if my grandfather happened to walk in. That distinguished gentleman's pride and joy, the pick of his vineyard, his better bottles, so temptingly labelled *'pour les grandes occasions'* and more eminently drinkable than the ordinary wine he normally produced, had a habit of disappearing from his *cave*, the wine-cellar cave next door. His temper was formidable and we were terrified of it – quite right too: after all, it was his house. But the kitchen never really seemed to be under his jurisdiction.

Cuisine grand-mère is traditional French home cooking, the repertoire of dishes that are eaten *en famille* and as party pieces, recipes handed down from grandmother to mother to daughter, collected on scraps of paper from relations and friends. The principle remains the same, but the communication systems change with the times. My sisters and I are quickly getting into the habit of swopping recipes by fax, and Clémence, my 9-year-old niece, makes us all feel very old when she jots down a recipe dictated over the phone to try it for herself . . .

This book is about French home cooking as I know it – the way my family cooked. My *cuisine grand-mère* is based on family recipes that I started collecting, and experimenting with,

The main approach to Fourchettes

nearly twenty years ago. Cooking proper began for me after leaving Oxford when I was let loose on my first kitchen in a basement flat in Shepherds Bush. My first graduate dinner party was a mitigated success. I scalded my ankle when I dropped a dish of braised celery (no one saw the mishap so back into the dish went the wretched vegetable). The evening was saved by Madeleine's *pommes meringuées*, a gorgeous triple-layered combination of tart apple slices at the bottom, thick, sweet *crème pâtissière* in the middle and crisp meringue on top.

Recipes in a family network are never particularly precise – a little glass of this and a handful of that, a pinch of this and two fingers' width of that – but battles can rage between relatives and friends about their different versions of the same dish. Do you really put mushrooms in your *boeuf bourguignon*, cheese in your *quiche lorraine*, croûtons around your *blanquette de veau*? If the dish is a success, the argument is forgotten and the revised version of the recipe – or some particularly good trick – may make its way in due course into a new set of files.

Cuisine grand-mère is not about authenticity at all cost. It always errs on the side of practicality. It loves making do, with the help of little twists that work well, clever *trucs*, not-so-secret family secrets proudly and willingly shared with others. It assumes that the recipients are not absolute beginners, but have a clue about basic techniques, enough common sense and a touch of flair. Given these not unreasonable assumptions, it is friendly and sensible, not aimed at experts but at amateurs who have to cook regularly and might as well get some satisfaction from it.

Sometimes it will cut corners, especially when it comes to daunting complex classics with dozens of obscure ingredients. Sensible editing takes place: the chances are – outside the South-West – that a family *cassoulet* will not quite be the 'real' thing, whatever that may be. But it will be practical, and will probably taste all right even if you are hundreds of miles from the Castelnaudary market. Last but not least it will not be extravagant.

Thrift is an important part of the *grand-mère* approach. My own grandmother enjoyed telling us, three-quarters jokingly, that we were lucky to have both butter and jam on our *tartines*: it wasn't like that in her day, one or the other, yes, but not both. That was a matter of principle.

A cave sitting room with frescoes

Cheaper cuts of meat are simmered for a long time, offal tackled uncompromisingly, vegetables and seasonal produce feature prominently when at their best and cheapest. I remember the astonishment on an American boyfriend's face when he was formally served a summer dinner of boiled egg (one or two, on request) followed by a mountain of *haricots verts* from the garden, tender, buttered and garlicky. Then came a local *Cendré* goat's cheese and, at the last, a large dish of strawberries, picked that afternoon, served with *crème fraîche* in honour of our guest. He asked me if my grandmother was a vegetarian – this was in the early Seventies, before vegetarian became a household word.

In the Seventies and during most of the Eighties, poor old *cuisine grand-mère* took quite a knocking. It was eclipsed by the clean lines and sharp colours of *nouvelle cuisine*. It lost the battle in bistros and homes *à la mode* (*grand-mère*, in any case, never claimed to be the cuisine of top restaurants), but patiently waited for the wheel to turn and upstart *nouvelle* to lose its youthful charm. And, after two decades, the age of *cuisine grand-mère* has clearly come again. Fashionable chefs everywhere are confiding that they have rediscovered the joys and values of

Lotte à la Provençale

> 750g de lotte
> 4 tomates ou 1 petite boîte
> 2 gros oignons
> 1 gousse d'ail
> 1 verre de vin blanc sec
> 6 cuillerés à soupe d'huile d'olive
> 50g de fromage râpé
> persil, thym, romarin, sel, poivre,

Coupez la lotte en morceaux. Faites-la revenir vivement à la poêle dans la moitié de l'huile d'olive avec l'oignon haché. Très vite la lotte deviendra plus ferme et d'un blanc doré. Retirez-la de la poêle, disposez-la dans un

T.S.V.P

Monkfish

Gratin dauphinois

> 750g de p. de terre
> 2 œufs
> ½ litre lait
> 2 1 gousses d'ail
> sel, poivre
> 50g de beurre

Coupez les p. de terre en rondelles assez fines. Disposez-les par rangée dans un plat à four, préalablement frotté avec une gousse d'ail puis beurré. Faites tiédir le lait, battez y les œufs avec sel poivre et une muscade. Versez ce mélange sur les p. de terre. Ajoutez qq morceaux de beurre à la surface. Cuisez à four chaud environ 45 min.

Potato gratin

Gratin de Haddock au riz

pour 4 personnes

> 750g de filets de haddock
> 1 L. de lait
> 50g de fromage râpé
> 1 œuf
> 250g riz
> sel, poivre, un muscade, persil
> 50g de beurre ou margarine
> 3 cuillerés de chapelure

Lavez les filets de haddock, mettez les à cuire à l'eau froide. Quand l'eau commence à bouillir égouttez le haddock, remettez à cuire à l'eau froide laissez frémir 5 minutes, égouttez, rincez bien finir de le peler X Puis mettez à cuire le haddock dans 1 L. de lait avec une cuillerés de beurre et

T.S.V.P

Smoked haddock

cuisine traditionnelle (a posh professional relative of both *grand-mère* and its fundamentalist country cousin, *cuisine du terroir*), while remembering the strong points of *nouvelle* – lightness, apparent simplicity and the use of the best possible ingredients.

The good-natured *grand-mère* approach is nothing if not flexible. It has reacted well to this new challenge, lost a few calories, worked on its looks and adopted some new tricks. Once again it is comfortably reigning in French kitchens – even if recipes have to be faxed during the cook's office hours.

Cuisine grand-mère is old-fashioned by definition. It assumes that the cook's place is in the house – not necessarily at the stove, but at hand: to give the pot a quick stir, add a few mushrooms twenty minutes before serving, then finish off the sauce with a nifty liaison. Rather than great skills it requires a little attention, and a presence. In the 1990's it makes perfect weekend cooking – relaxing but fiddly enough to be satisfying for the person who enjoys cooking. And it is ideal for the growing number of people who are chosing to work from home – what could be nicer than abandoning the desk for five minutes' creative pottering in the kitchen.

The end result will be satisfying too: there is nothing particularly *légère* about *cuisine grand-mère*. I have tried to make my recipes as light as possible without altering their character and have given options whenever I can. This was not too difficult an exercise as, perhaps not altogether by accident, thrifty often coincides with healthy in the *grand-mère* style as I know it. Starter salads and vegetables are used in abundance, and sweet desserts kept for special occasions. By tradition butter, cream and eggs are ingredients you are supposed to be reasonably economical with. Flour I use sparingly. Waste not, want not: this is not meanness but just good old household management. The French spend a great deal more of their income on food than the English or Americans, but they believe in spending their money wisely.

One other cost-conscious lesson that I try to heed is to make leftovers palatable – I am not saying that I use them creatively, because the idea of stretching *les restes* to the limit makes me shudder. Old habits die hard, however. As I write I am recovering from a surfeit of left-over Easter *gigot*. It was a joy served cold at the next meal, with a good garlic mayonnaise, and still pretty good the day after as a spicy *hachis parmentier* under a layer of creamed potato. But what was I to do on the third day? There was still a lot of *gigot* left. Well, I hesitated and looked at it, and thought of stuffed tomatoes and hesitated again. In the end, the dog Dickie had a great supper.

Absorbent paper: use liberally for drying ingredients and wiping hands, utensils and work surfaces.

beurre manié: mash together 1 teaspoon each of flour and soft butter. Divide into pellets and stir vigorously into hot sauces that need thickening over the heat.

butter: probably because I was brought up eating unsalted butter, I now really enjoy the taste of butter which is lightly salted. When a recipe does, however, demand soft unsalted butter, it is specified.

chicken stock: a light stock can easily be made by simmering the carcass, or at least some bones, and gizzards if possible, with a leek (or spring onion), carrot, bouquet garni (a sprig each of parsley and thyme and a bay leaf) for 30 minutes while you cook the meat. For a more elaborate method, see the *poule au pot recipe* (page 88). Chicken stock is worth having at hand in the freezer.

chinois: a narrow extremely fine sieve and a useful utensil to have.

citrus fruit: use unwaxed lemons and oranges, now available in many supermarkets, if you are going to zest them. Zest should really be blanched first in boiling water.

crème fraîche: double cream with a dash of lemon makes a most acceptable substitute.

eggs: I try to use free range eggs whenever possible. And, without being pious about it, it is a good idea to always break eggs separately into a small bowl or saucer. The, albeit rare, occasions when an egg is bad invariably happen when you've just broken the last of the ten required for a mammoth meringue . . .

fish stock: the quickest of all stocks to make, with fish bones, prawn or other crustacean shells, simmered in water for 10 minutes together with a bouquet garni.

food processor: invaluable, particularly for non-pastry cooks, but takes surprisingly long to be thoroughly at home with. I am on my mark 2 now, a Magimix *Cuisine Système 3000* and the whole business of thinking 'food processor' is only just becoming second nature.

garnish: should really be part of the dish rather than a last minute addition. I have not used the word in recipes.

herbs: I use fresh herbs extravagantly, particularly in mixed leaf salads, so I try to grow my own – as much as is feasible on a window sill. Supermarkets have started selling a good range of growing herbs (parsley, coriander, basil, chives, chervil) in little tubs which are much better value than pre-packed cut herbs. When in need I fall back on spring onions.

hollandaise: I now make mine in the food processor. Bring to the boil 4 teaspoons of white wine vinegar or lemon juice with 3 tablespoons of water. Season with freshly ground black pepper and reduce the mixture to about 2 teaspoons. Melt 150 g/5 oz/10 tablespoons unsalted butter in a separate saucepan until foamy – but do not allow to colour. Process 2 egg yolks with a small pinch of salt until smooth. Whizz in the reduced vinegar. With the machine on, trickle in the bubbling butter through the feed tube, a few drops at a time to begin with, then a little faster as the mixture starts to emulsify. Carry on until the sauce is smooth and thick. Check the seasoning and use as soon as possible – or keep for up to 30 minutes over warm water.

kitchen hygiene: I use a separate chopping board for raw meat and go through vast amounts of absorbent paper and disposable kitchen cloths. Teatowels are put in the wash extremely frequently, and tend to have a very short life.

lardons: these chunky little cubes of pork, usually from the smoked breast of the animal, are now sold vacuum-packed in French supermarkets and worth bringing back from a trip, so long as they travel in a cool bag. Otherwise, ask your local favourite delicatessen or butcher to sell you streaky bacon in thick 2.5 cm/1 in slices. Cut into small dice – the flavour and crunch they add to salads, quiches and other dishes – lentils in particular – will be much greater than if you simply snip a standard rasher.

mayonnaise: hard-to-resist lovely mayonnaise can be made the slow painful way, by hand with a wooden spoon – or painlessly whizzed in the food processor. I tend to compromise with an electric whisk. Once you have made sure that ingredients and equipment are all at the same (room) temperature, and promised yourself that on no account will you speed up the process and pour in the oil too fast, there remains the familiar problem of having only two hands. One hand is to trickle in the oil, and the other to handle the whisk. But what about the slippery bowl? I wedge it firmly in place on a mat of dampened kitchen cloth.

Much as I like olive oil, I do not recommend it using it on its own for mayonnaise – it will completely take over. Groundnut on its own is extremely bland, so I use the mix below. Serves 6.

2 medium-sized egg yolks

2 teaspoons wine vinegar (red or white)

a small pinch of salt

½ teaspoon Dijon mustard

150 ml/¼ pint/⅔ cup groundnut oil

120 ml/4 fl oz/½ cup light flavoured olive oil

To season

freshly ground black pepper

sea salt

lemon juice

To flavour

finely chopped herbs – chervil, chives, parsley, tarragon or watercress

finely chopped garlic

finely chopped gherkins

anchovy essence

Bring all the ingredients and equipment to room temperature.

Beat the egg yolks until combined, then beat in the vinegar, salt and mustard. Whisking constantly, trickle in the goundnut oil, literally drop by drop to begin, then a few drops at a time.

As soon as the mixture really appears to be thickening trickle in the oil just a little more continuously, still whisking. Carry on until you have incorporated both the groundnut and olive oils.

Now taste the mayonnaise and season it with freshly ground black pepper, extra salt, if you like, and a little lemon juice. Beat in 1 tablespoon of boiling water, this will help the mayonnaise keep stable. Cover with cling film and chill until needed. If you like, flavour to taste with some of the suggested additions.

measurements: these are expressed in metric, Imperial and American. Follow only one set.

microwave: I have one but never think of it as an adjunct to French-style home cooking.

oil: for reasons of space, I normally only keep groundnut oil and two kinds of olive oil, a light one and a very strong, top quality extra virgin brand – there are a great many to experiment with.

peeling: in the recipes I assume that garlic and onions are peeled as a matter of course. If other vegetables require peeling, this is specified.

salad spinner: a wonderful gadget that collects all the moisture from salad leaves and saves a great deal of time and energy. A modest investment which I thoroughly recommend.

sauce blanche: white sauce. This quick recipe is a useful starting point for many variations. As well as the additions I suggest, also try mustard and capers. Béchamel is made exactly in the same way, using milk instead of water. Flavour with tomato purée or cream and grated Gruyère. Serves 4.

550 ml/18 fl oz/2⅓ cups light stock or water

60 g/2 oz/4 tablespoons butter

60 g/2 oz/⅓ cup flour

sea salt

freshly ground black pepper

To enrich

30 g/1 oz/2 tablespoons or more butter, and/or the juice of 1 lemon

or 150 ml/¼ pint/⅔ cup *crème fraîche*

or 1 egg yolk and 90 ml/3 fl oz/⅓ cup single cream

In a heavy-based saucepan, over a moderate heat, melt the butter, then stir in the flour, using a wooden spoon. Moisten at once with a little of the stock or water, stir to mix – from this stage on, I use a balloon whisk. Add the rest of the liquid, still stirring. Bring slowly to a boil, whisking very frequently, then reduce the heat and cook for several minutes – this is important, otherwise the sauce will taste floury. Season to taste with sea salt and freshly ground black pepper.

Enrich the sauce with 30 g/1 oz/2 tablespoons or more butter and the juice of 1 lemon, or with 150 ml/¼ pint/⅔ cup *crème fraîche* just before serving. Alternatively, combine in a small bowl 1 large egg yolk and 90 ml/3 fl oz/⅓ cup single cream. Stir a little warm sauce into the egg and cream, then add to the pan and whisk in vigorously over the heat. Keep whisking hard until the sauce becomes creamy.

sauté pan: like all French home-cooks I use mine a great deal.

scissors: I keep several pairs of kitchen scissors and use them constantly, for snipping fresh herbs, spring onions, bacon rashers, etc. In the interests of hygiene, the scissors used for snipping raw meats are of a different colour.

sea salt: it tastes better than ordinary salt and you need less of it. The texture of coarse sea salt is particularly pleasant.

short cuts: in my experience the French have always

believed in using little tricks to make life easier and are no puritans when it comes to short cuts in the kitchen. I often use bought-in pastry and, now that it is at last on the market under the brand name of *Fonds de Cuisine*, bought-in good quality stocks. Expensive, but money wisely spent.

spatula: a good spatula should be heatproof and flexible. It is not an easy thing to find. The best one I ever had was a present from an American friend and I have never found its like in Britain or France.

things to bring back from France: my current shopping list includes vacuum-packed *lardons*, small blue-green *lentilles du Puy*, bitter dark chocolate, *saucisson*, small tins of extra fine flageolets, sugared ground almonds and potato peelers (to give as presents). I no longer bring back cheeses as most will not mature well after a bout of travelling.

timing: I find that even if I follow a recipe to the letter, the exact timing mysteriously varies from one occasion to the next. Always keep an eye on the progress and be prepared to take action and turn the heat up, down or off sooner – or later – than expected.

tomato *coulis:* a thin, sieved purée of the juice and pulp of either tinned or preferably, fresh ripe tomatoes. Infinitely better than tomato purée and much used in the French kitchen – and mine.

vinaigrette: often too acidic. Use only top quality vinegar and oil. A good basic vinaigrette is made with 1 tablespoon of red wine vinegar, 5 tablespoons of groundnut oil, a tiny quantity of mustard and a generous seasoning of sea salt and pepper. Stir vigorously with a small sauce whisk.

If like me, you eat large quantities of salad and like a thick and emulsified vinaigrette, follow my uncle Jean's method. Blend or process together 100 ml/3½ fl oz/generous ⅓ cup red wine vinegar, 600 ml/1 pint/2½ cups groundnut oil, 1 tablespoon of strong Dijon mustard, 2 teaspoons of salt and plenty of ground black pepper. Check the seasoning and refrigerate for 1 hour, then, blend or process again. Refrigerate in a tightly closed, impeccably clean jar. This vinaigrette will keep for up to three weeks.

SOUPE AU PISTOU
Vegetable Soup with Basil, Garlic and Cheese

POTAGE SAINT-GERMAIN/*Fresh Pea Soup*

SOUPE AUX LENTILLES/*Lentil Soup*

GRATINÉE AU ROQUEFORT
Onion Soup with Roquefort

POTAGE À L'OSEILLE/*Sorrel Soup*

POTAGE BONNE FEMME
Leek, Carrot and Potato Soup

POTAGE AU POTIRON/*Pumpkin Soup*

VICHYSSOISE AUX ASPERGES ET FINES HERBES
Asparagus and Herb Vichyssoise

SOUPE FRAÎCHE AUX EPINARDS ET À L'AVOCAT
Chilled Spinach and Avocado Soup

VELOUTÉ AUX CHAMPIGNONS
Creamy Mushroom Soup

Potages

Soups

A LARGE WHITE CHINA tureen in the centre of the table, fragrant steam, deep plates full of velvety goodness – my early memories of soup are of contentment and a feeling that things were as they should be and had always been. The curtains were drawn against the winter night, a clock was ticking somewhere. I was sharing an evening meal with my father's parents, *Bon-Papa* and *Bonne-Maman*, a quietly happy couple at peace with the world.

In France, as elsewhere, soup for a long time was the only dish at the last meal of the day. Hence the verb *souper* which meant just what it said – to take evening soup – centuries before it went upmarket to describe a late, light meal. Soup in French homes has remained an evening rather than a lunch-time dish, starter or main course, perhaps not quite as popular as it used to be, but making a distinct comeback now that more and more kitchens are equipped with that magic *robot*, the food processor. It seems that once again soup is good for you.

Soupe or *potage*? Most French people will tell you that the words are synonymous, but if you delve into it, *potage* turns out to be rather more refined, implying culinary skills, the use of a sieve or the making of a liaison. Soup started life humbly as a slice of stale bread over which hot liquid was poured. It has remained part of the French experience every bit as much as cheese: some decades ago Curnonsky listed over five hundred varieties of *soupes* and *potages*, from starry kitchens to farmhouses.

Soup is flexible and accommodating – the one thing it does suffer from is not being served hot enough. As I like a good substantial soup but not buckets of it, I have generally allowed in the recipes about 1.2l/2 pints/5 cups liquid for 4 servings. This is only a guideline, as many factors influence the water content of any given vegetable. Feel free to vary and add a little extra water, stock or cream if the soup seems too thick – or if you have an extra guest. It is a dish that can usually be stretched to go a little further.

Soupe au Pistou
Vegetable Soup with Basil, Garlic and Cheese

Pistou is what Genoa's *pesto* becomes along the coast, on the French side of the border. This big generous soup is well worth the entire crop of a kitchen pot of basil. Followed by a lightly dressed green salad, some cheese and a little fruit, it makes a good *plat unique* supper. And it has the advantage of being unobtrusively vegetarian – a good dish to serve to a mixed party. The meat-eaters won't miss their fix.

350 g/12 oz small white haricot beans

2 medium-sized potatoes

350 g/12 oz French beans

350 g/12 oz courgettes

2 carrots

2 leeks

1 turnip

sea salt

Serves 6–8

freshly ground black pepper

120 g/4 oz small macaroni

For the *pistou* sauce

2 ripe tomatoes

4–6 cloves of garlic

several sprigs of fresh basil

120 g/4 oz grated Parmesan

100 ml/3½ fl oz/generous ⅓ cup olive oil

60 g/2 oz/⅔ cup grated Gruyère, to serve

Soak the haricot beans overnight or for at least 6 hours. Drain. Put the haricots in a large saucepan, pour in 2.3 1/4 pints/9¼ cups cold water and bring to the boil. Skim if necessary.

While the haricots are beginning to cook, prepare the other vegetables. Peel and chop the potatoes, top and tail the beans, then cut into segments, slice the courgettes, scrape or peel the carrots, then slice and wash the leeks, peel and chop the turnip. Make sure the vegetable pieces are roughly the same size and no larger than 4 cm/1½ in.

After ½ an hour add the vegetables to the pan, cover and simmer for 1 hour, or until the haricots and vegetables are cooked. Season lightly with salt and freshly ground black pepper. Trickle in the macaroni and finish cooking the soup, uncovered.

Meanwhile, prepare the *pistou* sauce. Blanch, skin, seed and chop the tomatoes. Using a large pestle and mortar, pound the garlic, then add the basil leaves and pound well. Work in the chopped tomatoes and half the Parmesan, then add the olive oil a little at a time, mixing it in as for a mayonnaise. Alternatively, combine everything in the food processor, taking care not to over-process the mixture. Stir 1 ladleful of the soup liquid into the sauce, then pour into the soup and leave to settle and infuse for a few minutes over a low heat.

Combine the remaining Parmesan with the Gruyère and serve in a bowl at the same time as the soup.

POTAGE SAINT-GERMAIN
Fresh Pea Soup

A DELICATE PEA SOUP flavoured with chervil. The *Saint-Germain* in question is the *Comte de Saint-Germain*, Louis XV's war minister, whose name blesses preparations involving peas. Reduce the amount of water to 250 ml/8 fl oz/1 cup in the recipe below, go easy on the blending and, *voilà*, you have *purée Saint-Germain*, a good accompaniment to fish and veal.

	Serves 4	
750 g/1½ lb fresh baby garden peas, in the pod		60 ml/4 tablespoons/¼ cup single cream
hearts of 3 lettuces	a few sprigs of parsley	sea salt
12 button onions	90 g/3 oz/6 tablespoons butter	freshly ground black pepper
several sprigs of chervil	1 small egg yolk	small croûtons, to serve

SHELL THE PEAS, SHRED THE LETTUCE hearts, chop the onions and snip the fresh herbs. In a large heavy-based saucepan, heat 60 g/2 oz/4 tablespoons butter, then add the vegetables and herbs, and cook gently for 5 minutes, stirring frequently.

Pour in 1.2 1/2 pints/5 cups boiling water and simmer for 20–30 minutes, until the vegetables are very tender. Reserving 2–3 tablespoons of peas, transfer the vegetables and most of the liquid to a blender or food processor. Blend until smooth and return to the pan. Alternatively, push through a fine sieve, mashing the vegetables well with the back of a wooden spoon to extract as much pulp as possible. Whisk the liquid and purée until well combined.

Reheat gently. Combine the egg yolk and cream in a small bowl, stir in a little soup, then gradually add this liaison to the pan, stirring well. Season to taste with salt and freshly ground black pepper. Just before serving, stir in the reserved peas, whisk in the remaining butter and add the croûtons.

SOUPE AUX LENTILLES
Lentil Soup

Lᴇɴᴛɪʟs sᴇᴇᴍ ᴛᴏ be to the early 1990's what the kiwi fruit was to the previous decade – and after years of neglect, it is now a case of lentils with practically everything. As a lifelong loyal supporter of these pulses, I am delighted to see them back in fashion. For me, no trip to France is complete without the purchase of at least one packet of dark green little *lentilles du Puy*. They cook quickly and cleanly, without disintegrating into an unappetising mush, and they have a good strong flavour.

	Serves 4	
450 g/1 lb small dark green lentils		1 thick-cut rasher smoked bacon, without the rind
2 tablespoons olive oil, plus extra for serving, if wished	1 large onion	bouquet garni
	1 clove of garlic	1 tablespoon tomato purée
30 g/1 oz/2 tablespoons butter, plus extra for serving, if wished	1 large potato	sea salt
	1 carrot	freshly ground black pepper

Rɪɴsᴇ ᴛʜᴇ ʟᴇɴᴛɪʟs ᴡᴇʟʟ ᴀɴᴅ sᴏᴀᴋ ᴛʜᴇᴍ for 10 minutes in fresh cold water. Meanwhile, gently heat the oil and butter in a large heavy-based saucepan, and prepare the vegetables.

Chop the onion and garlic, peel and chop the potato, scrape or peel then slice the carrot. Sauté the onion in the pan until browned, then add the drained lentils and the vegetables. Chop up the bacon and add to the pan. Stir until everything is well mixed.

Add the bouquet garni and about 1.5 l/2½ pints/6 cups cold water to the pan. Bring gently to the boil and simmer for about half an hour or until the lentils and vegetables are cooked and soft. Reserving about 2 ladlefuls, blend the soup in a blender or food processor. Return to the pan, stir in the reserved unblended mixture and the tomato purée. If the soup looks too thick, thin it down with a cup of boiling water.

Season to taste with salt and freshly ground black pepper. Serve piping hot. You may like to add a trickle of olive oil or a knob of butter to each bowl of soup.

Any left-over soup will keep very nicely in the refrigerator for a couple of days – just remember to add a little extra liquid when reheating.

GRATINÉE AU ROQUEFORT
Onion Soup with Roquefort

A CHEESE LOVER's version of the celebrated soup. It is gutsy, simple and effective – a good dish to 'delegate'
to would-be helping hands, but make sure they don't burn the onions.
For a luxurious finishing touch, try spooning a little liaison of egg yolk and cream into each bowl,
in between the top crust and the soup. Definitely not home fare as I remember it, but recently enjoyed
in a London restaurant.

Serves 4

750 g/1½ lb large white onions

90 g/3 oz/6 tablespoons butter

2 teaspoons flour

sea salt

freshly ground black pepper

a little nutmeg, grated or
ground

2–3 tablespoons brandy

120 g/4 oz Roquefort

8–12 thin slices French bread

30 g/1 oz Gruyère

SLICE THE ONIONS FAIRLY THINLY. IN A large heavy-based saucepan, melt the butter and gently sauté the onion slices until soft, without letting them colour. Sprinkle over the flour and stir in well. Pour in 1.2 1/2 pints/5 cups boiling water and cook for 15–20 minutes. Heat the oven to 200°C/400°F/Gas 6. Season the soup with salt, freshly ground black pepper, a little nutmeg and brandy.

Mash the Roquefort with a fork. Reserve 4 slices of French bread and spread the mashed Roquefort over the rest. Arrange the coated bread in individual ovenproof bowls, then pour in the soup. Place a slice of the reserved bread on top of each serving, then grate the Gruyère over the top.

Brown in the oven for about 10 minutes and serve at once.

Potage à l'Oseille
Sorrel Soup

Fresh, green and a little sharp, this is a lovely spring soup. Once the sorrel spell is over, I use exactly the same method to make watercress or spinach soup.

450 g/1 lb sorrel

30 g/1 oz/2 tablespoons butter

2 potatoes

1 egg yolk

Serves 4

90 ml/3 fl oz/⅓ cup double cream

sea salt

freshly ground black pepper

Wash, trim and roughly shred the sorrel leaves. In a large heavy-based saucepan, melt the butter, add the sorrel leaves and gently stew for a few minutes.

Meanwhile, peel the potatoes and cut into rough 2.5 cm/1 in dice. Add to the sorrel, pour in 1.2 1/2 pints/5 cups cold water, bring to the boil and cook for a further 10–15 minutes. In a small bowl, combine the egg yolk and the cream, stirring in the cream gradually. Keep aside.

Transfer the soup mixture to a blender or food processor, reserving a few tablespoons of the liquid. Blend the soup. Stir the reserved liquid into the egg and cream. Return the soup to the pan, then gradually add the egg and cream, whisking well. Season to taste, then reheat until very hot, but do not boil.

Potage Bonne Femme
Leek, Carrot and Potato Soup

A simple and comforting soup. I have tried finishing it off with a dollop of *crème fraîche*, but have gone back to using butter which somehow always tastes better with root vegetables.

2 waxy potatoes

3 largish leeks

4 carrots

90 g/3 oz/6 tablespoons butter, plus extra for serving

Serves 4

a few sprigs of fresh thyme

2 bay leaves

1–2 cloves of garlic, peeled

sea salt

freshly ground black pepper

Peel the potatoes, wash and trim the leeks, then scrape or peel the carrots. Chop the vegetables into rough 2.5 cm/1 in cubes. In a heavy-based saucepan, melt half the butter, then sauté the vegetables until lightly coloured. Add the thyme, bay leaves and garlic to the vegetables, then pour in about 1.2 1/2 pints/ 5 cups boiling water. Simmer for about half an hour.

When the vegetables are cooked, blend the soup in the blender or food processor. Season to taste with salt and freshly ground black pepper. Serve piping hot, with a good knob of butter in each bowl.

POTAGE AU POTIRON
Pumpkin Soup

Wᴉᴛʜ ᴛʜᴇ ᴇxᴄᴇᴘᴛɪᴏɴ of courgettes, the favoured baby of the family, gourds and squashes do not feature very highly on the list of prized French vegetables. Pumpkins, in particular, have a lowly status and are often regarded as cattle fodder. However, they are discreetly put to very good use in a number of tasty country soups, like my autumnal favourite below.

Serves 4

450 g/1 lb wedge of pumpkin

2 large ripe tomatoes

1 large white onion

60 g/2 oz/4 tablespoons butter

1 scant tablespoon sugar

1.2 l/2 pints/5 cups milk

sea salt

freshly ground black pepper

60 ml/4 tablespoons/¼ cup single cream

a few sprigs of parsley

croûtons, to serve

Rᴇᴍᴏᴠᴇ ᴛʜᴇ sᴋɪɴ ᴀɴᴅ sᴇᴇᴅs ꜰʀᴏᴍ ᴛʜᴇ pumpkin. Dice the flesh. Blanch, skin and seed the tomatoes, then chop the flesh. Coarsely chop the onion. In a large, heavy-based saucepan, melt half the butter, then stir in the vegetables and cook for a couple of minutes. Sprinkle in the sugar and add a small glass of water. Cover and cook gently for about 30 minutes, or until all the vegetables are soft.

Meanwhile, bring the milk to the boil in a suitable saucepan, then keep hot. Add half the milk to the cooked vegetables and blend, using a blender or food processor, then pour the mixture into the pan with the remaining hot milk and whisk in. Alternatively, push the purée through a sieve into the hot milk and whisk in vigorously until well combined.

Season to taste with salt and freshly ground black pepper, then stir in the cream. Keep the soup hot over a gentle heat. Snip the parsley. Just before serving, whisk in the remaining butter.

Sprinkle on the croûtons and the snipped parsley as preferred.

VICHYSSOISE AUX ASPERGES ET FINES HERBES
Asparagus and Herb Vichyssoise

ASPARAGUS PRICES VARY ENORMOUSLY . . . this is a soup I make as soon as the precious stalks have lost their early season novelty appeal, when their cost has come down to that of run of the mill vegetables. This is not a difficult dish to make, but its texture and appearance will be much enhanced if you (a) conscientiously prepare the asparagus, removing all the strings, and (b) sweat the onions over a very low heat to prevent them from browning. Consume hot or chilled, depending on the weather. When I serve this vichyssoise chilled, these days I often finish it off with Greek-style yoghurt rather than cream, but *yaourt* definitely did not feature in my original recipe.

the white parts of 4 large spring onions

1 large potato

500 g/1 lb bunch of asparagus

40 g/1½ oz/3 tablespoons butter

1.2 l/2 pt/5 cups chicken stock (see page 12)

Serves 4

several sprigs each of tarragon and chives

a small bunch of chervil

sea salt

freshly ground black pepper

125 ml/5 fl oz/½ cup single cream (or a mixture of cream and yoghurt, see above)

PREPARE THE VEGETABLES. PEEL AND finely slice the onions. Peel and chop the potato. Carefully trim the asparagus, discarding any tough woody ends and peeling off any knobbly, stringy bits. Cut and reserve the tips of 4–12 stalks (depending on size). Cut the remaining stalks into segments.

In a large heavy-based saucepan, melt the butter over a low heat. Add the sliced onions and sweat for a few minutes, stirring frequently and keeping the heat low so that the onions do not colour. Add the chopped potato and continue stirring for a few minutes, still over a low heat.

Add the asparagus segments to the onions and potato, pour in the stock and gently bring to a simmer. Snip in half the tarragon, chives and chervil into the mixture and season lightly with salt and freshly ground black pepper. Now cover and simmer gently for about 20 minutes until the asparagus and potato are soft.

Add the reserved asparagus tips after about 15 minutes. Remove the asparagus tips from the pan and set aside. Leave the soup to cool for a few minutes, then liquidise or process. If the texture looks less than perfectly smooth, press the soup through a fine sieve. Check the seasoning.

If serving hot, pour the soup back into the pan, stir in the cream and heat through gently. Snip in the remaining herbs, stir them into the soup, then add the reserved asparagus tips at the last minute.

If serving chilled, stir in half the cream and 4 tablespoons cold water – the soup tends to thicken as it gets cold. Leave the soup until cold and refrigerate for at least 2 hours or until needed. Also chill the reserved asparagus tips. Just before serving, check the seasoning, snip in the remaining herbs and stir well in. Swirl in the remaining cream and plop in a few ice cubes, then add the asparagus tips.

Soupe Fraîche aux Epinards et à l'Avocat

Chilled Spinach and Avocado Soup

WHENEVER I CAN find baby spinach and decent avocados in the market at the same time, usually for a month or so in the early summer – and sometimes again at the very end of that season – this soup features regularly on the menu. The nutty smoothness of the avocado combines well with the slightly peppery sharpness of the spinach.

750 g/1½ lb young tender spinach	Serves 4	a few sprigs of flat-leafed parsley
sea salt		hot pepper sauce, cayenne pepper or *harissa*
3 ripe, blemish-free avocados		
2–3 lemons		

DISCARD THE SPINACH STALKS AND ANY large veiny ribs. Blanch in lightly salted boiling water for a couple of minutes. Drain. Meanwhile, skin and chop the avocados. Transfer them to a blender or food processor, squeeze the lemons and add the juice, then the wilted spinach. Snip the parsley and add to the avocado and spinach mixture. Blend. Add about 600 ml/1 pint/2½ cups water and blend again.

Transfer to a large bowl. Season to taste with salt and a little hot pepper sauce, cayenne pepper or *harissa*.

Gradually whisk in about 450 ml/¾ pint/ 2 cups water and perhaps a little extra lemon juice, until the soup has a nice consistency.

Refrigerate for at least 1 hour or until needed. Serve with a couple of ice cubes in each bowl.

Velouté aux Champignons
Creamy Mushroom Soup

Observant readers will notice that this is one of the few times that I use chicken stock in a soup recipe instead of plain *château la pompe* (tap water). The reason is that it makes a big difference to the flavour of the dish – one of those occasions when faking it with a stock cube just won't do.

Which type of mushroom to use? Any cultivated, very fresh mushrooms will give of their best in this recipe. At the moment I am favouring brown cap *champignons de Paris*. If you feel extravagant, follow a great *gourmand*'s advice: Curnonsky concludes his splendidly creamy version of *potage aux champignons* with the observation that the soup 'will obviously taste better with wild mushrooms'.

Serves 4

350 g/12 oz fresh mushrooms

½ lemon

90 g/3 oz/6 tablespoons butter, plus extra to finish

30 g/2 oz/⅓ cup flour

1.2 l/2 pints/5 cups chicken stock (see page 12)

1 or 2 egg yolks

100 ml/3½ fl oz/generous ⅓ cup double cream

sea salt

freshly ground black pepper

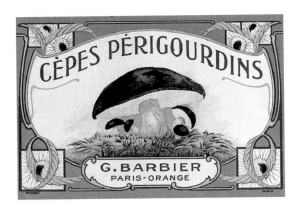

Wipe and trim the mushrooms. Keep aside 90 g/3 oz, and very finely chop the rest. Finely grate the zest of the lemon, then squeeze the juice, reserving both. In a large heavy-based saucepan, make a roux. Melt 60 g/2 oz/4 tablespoons of the butter, stir in the flour and cook gently for a couple of minutes, stirring constantly. Gradually pour in the chicken stock, a little at a time, stirring vigorously to prevent lumps forming, then add the chopped mushrooms and bring to the boil, still stirring. Reduce the heat and add the lemon juice and zest. Cook gently for a good 20–25 minutes, stirring frequently.

Meanwhile, slice the reserved mushrooms very finely and sauté in the remaining butter. In a small bowl, combine the egg yolk or yolks with the cream. Stir in a ladleful of the soup liquid, then gradually pour the mixture into the pan, stirring well. Keep hot but not boiling. Add the sautéed mushroom slices. Season to taste with salt and a little freshly ground black pepper. Whisk in a good knob of butter and serve piping hot.

POIREAUX VINAIGRETTE / *Leek Salad*

SALADE DE POIVRONS À L'AVOCAT
Sweet Red Pepper and Avocado Salad

CHAMPIGNONS EN SALADE
Mushroom Salad

CONCOMBRES À LA CRÈME
Creamy Cucumber Salad

CÉLERI RÉMOULADE / *Celeriac Mayonnaise*

SALADE DE TOMATES / *Tomato Salad*

TAPENADE / *Black Olive Purée*

ANCHOÏADE / *Anchovy Purée*

ROUILLE / *Provençal Hot Pepper Sauce*

ŒUFS MIMOSA
Hard-boiled Eggs with Anchovy Mayonnaise

MELONS RAFRAÎCHIS AU VIN DOUX
Chilled Melons with Sweet Wine

MACÉDOINE DE LÉGUMES FRAIS À LA MAYONNAISE
Fresh Vegetable Medley with Mayonnaise

CHOU EN SALADE
Shredded Cabbage Salad

CAROTTES RÂPÉES / *Grated Carrot Salad*

Hors d'Oeuvre

APPETISERS

No FRENCH FAMILY lunch is complete without some little *hors d'œuvre*, a clever starter that somehow simultaneously whets the appetite, yet takes the edge off it, while giving one a few extra minutes to organise the main dish. Most *hors d'œuvre* are as easy on the cook as they are appetising: many favourites need very little preparation indeed. What could be simpler to assemble than a few slices of *saucisson*, some black olives and wedges of hard-boiled egg? The dish welcomes you to the table without being in the least fussy.

My sister, Françoise, recently dampened my enthusiastic *hors d'œuvre* reminiscences by pointing out that the slices of *saucisson* were carefully counted and pre-prandial looting severely monitored. How could I forget . . . *Saucissons*, expensive and, even in a less health-conscious decade, not known for their dietary qualities, never lasted long in our house. More often than not, the *saucisson* ration was accompanied by a substantial fresh salad. This varied subtly according to the people sitting around the table. It could be marinated mushrooms when a friend of our mother came to lunch, creamy cucumber for grandparents and older relatives, or celeriac mayonnaise on the rare occasions our father managed to get away from the office. And if it was 'just us', something like plain grated carrots or shredded cabbage would be the order of the day.

POIREAUX VINAIGRETTE
Leek Salad

THE POOR MAN'S asparagus, the modest leek, really responds to being treated like its posh cousin. It is important to dress the leeks while they are still warm to let the flavours combine, and this starter is best eaten *tiède* – just above room temperature.

Serves 4

750 g/1½ lb fairly slim leeks

sea salt

a few sprigs of chives

FOR THE VINAIGRETTE

1 small hard-boiled egg

1 tablespoon Dijon mustard

sea salt

freshly ground black pepper

2 teaspoons white wine vinegar

about 90 ml/3 fl oz/⅓ cup groundnut oil

CUT OFF THE BEARDY ROOTS OF THE LEEKS and the tough end of the green tops. Slit the whole length of each leek with a sharp knife, working from the outside towards the centre and discard any discoloured top layers. Gently open the leeks and rinse well under cold running water. Tie the leeks in bunches of 3 or 4 and cook in boiling salted water for 8–10 minutes. Transfer to a large sieve or colander and drain well.

While the leeks are cooking, prepare the vinaigrette. Grate the hard-boiled egg into a small bowl, and mash with the mustard. Add a pinch of salt and a sprinkling of freshly ground black pepper, then stir in the vinegar and oil. Beat until well combined.

Gently squeeze the warm leeks with a very clean tea-towel to remove excess moisture. Arrange on a dish like asparagus and pour on the vinaigrette, then snip the chives and scatter on top. Sprinkle over a little extra pepper at the last minute and eat while still slightly warm.

SALADE DE POIVRONS À L'AVOCAT
Sweet Red Pepper and Avocado Salad

THIS COLOURFUL LITTLE starter has been a family favourite ever since avocados lost their *de luxe* dinner-party status and became staple fare for much of the year. Skinning peppers is a tedious task, so once I get going I always char more than I need for the salad: marinated peppers will mature nicely in the refrigerator for a week or so.

After a few days, you'll have a deep, piquant-sweet mixture that makes a good pasta sauce. Marinated peppers also do wonders for plain chicken pieces. Skin the chicken pieces, coat with the mixture and season generously with black pepper. Bake gently for 30–45 minutes, in a low oven, basting once.

Serves 4–6

3 ripe unblemished red peppers

90 ml/3 fl oz/⅓ cup good strong olive oil

2 ripe avocados

1 lemon

sea salt

freshly ground black pepper

crusty bread, to serve

WASH AND DRY THE PEPPERS, THEN CHAR them. I do that under the grill, cursing quietly as I burn my fingers, turning the peppers over until all the surfaces are charred and blistered. Leave them until cool enough to handle, and then remove the skins – they will peel off easily if the peppers are charred enough. Don't worry about small stubborn patches of skin – the marinade will soften them.

Cut the peppers in half lengthways and carefully remove the seeds, core and membrane. Slice into narrow strips and cut each strip into 2 or 3 segments. Put the peppers in a bowl, coat with the olive oil, cover with cling film and chill for at least 12 hours, during which time the mixture should be stirred once or twice.

Just before serving, halve the avocados, remove the stones and skin. Cut into neat pieces or thin slices, squeeze the lemon and moisten the avocados well with the juice. Combine with two-thirds of the marinated peppers and their juices, reserving the rest (see above).

Season with a very little salt and more generously with black pepper. Serve with crusty fresh bread.

CHAMPIGNONS EN SALADE
Mushroom Salad

THIS LIGHTLY MARINATED salad makes a neat, fresh little starter and is a good way of making the most of not very exciting cultivated mushrooms. It will keep well for a couple of days in the refrigerator.

350 g/12 oz fresh white button mushrooms	Serves 4	sea salt
1½ lemons		freshly ground black pepper
60 ml/4 tablespoons/¼ cup olive oil		a few sprigs of fresh parsley

TRIM ANY SANDY STALKS OFF THE mushrooms. Squeeze the lemons, then pour one-third of the juice into a bowl of cold water. Wash the mushrooms in the acidulated water. Dry them well with absorbent paper or a clean tea-towel, then slice them thinly straight into a salad bowl.

Stir in the remaining lemon juice, then trickle in the olive oil and stir until the mushroom slices are well coated. Season to taste with salt and freshly ground black pepper. Leave to stand in a cool place for a couple of hours. Before serving, finely chop the parsley and stir into the salad.

CONCOMBRES À LA CRÈME
Creamy Cucumber Salad

TO DEGORGE OR not to degorge – that is not the question, not for me, anyway, I am a de-gorger. But in terms of home-cooking, this is one of the great differences between French and Anglo-Saxon approaches. Generally speaking, the French always sprinkle cucumber flesh with salt, press it down with a weighted plate, and let it 'sweat' its excess moisture and bitter juices for half an hour. The texture and flavour will be distinctly finer.

2 cucumbers	Serves 4	150 ml/¼ pint/⅔ cup single cream
coarse sea salt		
a few sprigs of fresh tarragon		freshly ground black pepper
1 lemon		

WASH AND DRY (BUT DON'T PEEL) THE cucumbers. Run the prongs of a fork down the whole surface of each cucumber, then slice as thinly as you can, preferably with a mandolin or, alternatively, with a very sharp knife. Transfer the slices to a large sieve or colander and sprinkle with coarse salt. Place a plate or saucer on top of the cucumber slices and put a weight on it. Leave to stand for about 30 minutes.

Rinse thoroughly under cold running water. Pat dry conscientiously with absorbent paper or a clean tea-towel. Transfer the cucumber slices to a bowl. Snip the tarragon leaves into the bowl, squeeze the lemon, then pour in the juice and mix well. Gradually spoon in the cream, mixing it well into the salad. Season lightly with freshly ground black pepper, and refrigerate for at least 1 hour before serving. This salad is best eaten chilled.

CÉLERI RÉMOULADE
Celeriac Mayonnaise

A CREAMY-CRUNCHY traditional starter. *Sauce rémoulade* is a mayonnaise variation that is strong on mustard, and normally includes capers, gherkins and sometimes anchovy. I am not alone in leaving the last three powerful ingredients out of this recipe.

Serves 4

1–2 celeriac roots, about
450 g/1 lb total weight

1 lemon

salt

FOR THE *SAUCE RÉMOULADE*

1 egg yolk

2 tablespoons strong Dijon
mustard

1 teaspoon white wine vinegar

250 ml/8 fl oz/1 cup groundnut
oil

sea salt

freshly ground black pepper

a few sprigs of fresh parsley,
tarragon and chervil

paprika

PEEL AND GRATE THE CELERIAC ROOTS, then squeeze over the juice of the lemon and blanch in boiling salted water for a few minutes. Drain well in a large sieve or colander, squeeze out the excess moisture with your hands and leave to cool.

Meanwhile prepare the sauce. Mix together in a bowl the egg yolk, mustard and wine vinegar until well combined, then trickle in the oil, a few drops at a time to start, while whisking vigorously. You should end up with a thick mayonnaise – see page 13. Season with

salt and freshly ground black pepper. If the mayonnaise seems too solid, whisk in a tablespoon of boiling water. Finely snip the fresh herbs and stir into the sauce. Chill until ready to use.

Transfer to a serving bowl and stir in the dressing, a spoonful at a time – the celeriac should be evenly coated. Leave to chill for 1 hour at the very least, giving the salad an occasional stir.

Check the dressing before serving. Sprinkle on a little paprika, and extra snipped herbs.

Salade de Tomates
Tomato Salad

This is the simplest of starters, and one of the best, if – and that's a pretty hefty 'if' – it is made with the right tomatoes. The right tomatoes are fragrant and firm-fleshed, juicy but not watery, and ripe but not mushy. The size doesn't matter all that much, but I am suspicious of giants, particularly in this country. Make a note of the recipe and save for a sunny day and the perfect tomatoes.

450 g/1 lb 'proper' tomatoes

2 shallots or ½ large white onion, if preferred

a few sprigs of fresh parsley and chives

60 ml/4 tablespoons/¼ cup strong olive oil

Serves 4

2 teaspoons white wine vinegar

sea salt

freshly ground black pepper

To serve

fresh bread

black olives

Slice the tomatoes reasonably thinly and remove the core, seeds and a little of the pulp. Arrange in concentric circles on a round platter, working towards the centre.

Thinly slice the shallots or onion and scatter the rings or half-rings over the tomatoes. Snip the parsley and chives and then scatter over the dish.

Whisk together the olive oil and vinegar, then season with sea salt and a little black pepper. Sprinkle the dressing over the salad as evenly as possible. Leave to stand for 15 minutes or so before you eat – it will taste infinitely better at room temperature. Mop up the juices with plenty of fresh bread and have a bowl of black olives on the table.

Tapenade
Black Olive Purée

A RELAXING APÉRITIF is the best prelude to an enjoyable meal. And no proper apéritif is complete without some homemade *amuse-gueule*, a tasty little 'palate-tickler' that will keep everybody happy even if they have to wait for a late fellow-guest or a problematic dish. *Tapenade* served with croûtons is a summer favourite and much to be recommended with a glass of flinty cold Provence Rosé, or Pastis, if you prefer. Combine with croûtons spread with *rouille* (see page 36) for colour contrast – and memories of the Mediterranean.

120 g/4 oz fleshy black olives, stoned

1–2 cloves of garlic

a little fresh thyme, summer savory and coriander leaf

Serves 4

strong olive oil

1 small anchovy fillet in oil optional

freshly ground black pepper

CHOP UP THE OLIVES AND CRUSH THE garlic. Discard the stalks of the fresh herbs and shred the leaves. Pound together the olives, garlic and herbs, using a pestle and mortar, gradually adding olive oil until you have a thick smoothish paste.

Cut up and mash the anchovy fillet, then work it into the paste, adding more olive oil. Taste and season with freshly ground black pepper. Alternatively, whizz all the ingredients together in the food processor – check the taste before seasoning.

Anchoïade
Anchovy Purée

ANCHOÏADE CAN BE served cold, with crudités, or hot, spread over bread and toasted. There are many versions of this dish from Provence. My old favourite family recipe comes, I believe, from Draguignan.

225 g/8 oz salted anchovies, or 120 g/4 oz canned anchovy fillets in oil

2–4 cloves of garlic

1 tablespoon white wine vinegar

Serves 4

1 small hard-boiled egg

¼ large white onion

250 ml/8 fl oz/1 cup olive oil

freshly ground black pepper

thick slices of bread, to serve

IF YOU ARE USING SALTED ANCHOVIES, rinse them well under cold running water, then soak in fresh cold water for at least 1 hour, changing the water a couple of times. If using canned anchovies, drain off the oil.

Combine the anchovies with the garlic, vinegar, hard-boiled egg and onion in the food processor, then gradually work in three-quarters of the olive oil, reserving a little oil for later. If you are not using a food processor,

chop up the anchovies and garlic very finely, and combine with the vinegar. Chop up the egg and onion very finely too, and stir into the anchovy mixture until well combined. Beat in the olive oil a little at a time, as for a mayonnaise.

Spread the anchovy purée over thick slices of bread. Sprinkle on the remaining olive oil and season liberally with black pepper. Pop under the grill for a few minutes and serve hot.

ROUILLE
Provençal Hot Pepper Sauce

Rouille gets its name from its attractive rust colour, and its fieriness from small red hot peppers. With *tapenade* and *anchoïade* (see page 35), it makes an appetising trilogy. Serve with an assortment of raw vegetables, steamed or boiled small new potatoes, or spread on warm toasted bread.

	Serves 4	
2 small red chilli peppers		1 teaspoon tomato purée
2 cloves of garlic		100 ml/3½ fl oz/generous ⅓ cup olive oil
1 small slice stale white bread, crust removed	1 egg yolk	
a little milk	sea salt	cayenne pepper, if wished

Discard the stems and seeds of the chillies (soak dried peppers in cold water first for a few hours). Soak the bread in a little milk, then squeeze to get rid of excess milk.

Using a blender, food processor or pestle and mortar, combine or mash together the peppers, garlic, milky bread, egg yolk, salt and tomato purée. Add the oil a little at a time until the mixture is quite thick and smooth. Thin it out with a dash of cold water.

Check the seasoning – if it's not hot enough for you, sprinkle over a little cayenne pepper.

OEUFS MIMOSA
Hard-boiled Eggs with Anchovy Mayonnaise

A colourful starter which looks good on a buffet or party platter.

Serves 4

4 large eggs	a few sprigs of parsley	2 teaspoons anchovy essence
90 ml/3 fl oz/⅓ cup well seasoned mayonnaise (see page 13)	2 ripe tomatoes	2 anchovy fillets in oil
	1 cos lettuce	freshly ground black pepper

Boil the eggs for 10 minutes or so, then immerse in cold water until cool enough to shell. Meanwhile, prepare the mayonnaise (see page 13) and the other ingredients. Finely snip the parsley and slice the tomatoes, discarding the seeds and whitish core – you'll need 8 slices. Tear out, rinse and pat dry 8–10 presentable lettuce leaves.

Shell the hard-boiled eggs and halve them lengthways. Carefully remove the yolks with a teaspoon. Reserve 2 yolks. Using a fork, mash the other yolks with the anchovy essence, then combine with half the finely snipped parsley and the mayonnaise. Spoon the egg mayonnaise into the halved egg white cases. Trim the base of each a little if it looks wobbly.

Arrange the lettuce leaves and tomato slices on a platter, then place a stuffed half-egg on each tomato slice. Cut each anchovy fillet into 2 strips, and place over each egg in a cross.

Grate the reserved egg yolks over the dish – this is the mimosa effect. Sprinkle on the remaining parsley and a little black pepper. Refrigerate until ready to serve.

MELONS RAFRAÎCHIS AU VIN DOUX
Chilled Melons with Sweet Wine

Jᴜsᴛ ʟɪᴋᴇ ᴘᴇᴀʀs and Camembert, melons are quite unpredictable. You can make sure you select a ripe melon by choosing a fruit with a good heavy feel to it. It should give a little around the stalk and at the opposite end.

And if it is a Charentais or Cavaillon melon, it should also smell fruitily fragrant. Infuriatingly, not every carefully chosen melon delivers. For informal meals, I always taste a sliver of each melon and make sure every plate has a wedge of the day's glorious best and disappointing worst – no favouritism. For grander occasions, I go back to the old family special below. I was delighted to notice recently that it seemed to be a popular summer dish in Anjou and Touraine restaurants – with the flesh carefully pressed into melon balls, of course, but that's definitely not a trick *maison*.

Serves 4

**2 × 450 g/1 lb promising
Charentais or Cavaillon
melons, or 4 smaller Ogen
melons**

**½ bottle chilled sweet white
wine (Coteaux du Layon,
Vouvray doux or Beaumes de
Venise)**

**freshly ground black pepper, if
wished**

Hᴀʟᴠᴇ ᴛʜᴇ ᴍᴇʟᴏɴs ᴀɴᴅ sᴄᴏᴏᴘ ᴏᴜᴛ ᴛʜᴇ seeds and any membrane. If you are using small Ogen melons, remove the stalk end. Trim the bases if necessary so that the melon 'cups' stand upright. Refrigerate for at least 40 minutes.

To serve, pour a little chilled wine into each cup – the equivalent of a small glass. Float an ice cube or two on top and serve at once. For a special finishing touch, try it also with a little sprinkling of black pepper around the rim of each melon cup.

MACÉDOINE DE LÉGUMES FRAIS À LA MAYONNAISE
Fresh Vegetable Medley with Mayonnaise

A SUBSTANTIAL STARTER, popular with people who prefer their vegetables cooked. Add hard-boiled eggs, left-over strips of meat, fish and shellfish, and you have *salade Russe*. Both dishes are pleasing when homemade, but best avoided in unknown commercial establishments.
Canned *macédoine* is simply poor convenience food.
I used to wonder what, if anything, Alexander The Great of Macedonia had to do with this particular dish (is he not linked with another dish, the early form of sorbet he fatally consumed during a long banquet after battle?) . . . The answer was somewhat far-fetched. The *Petit Robert* dictionary, in a moment of levity, explains that *macédoine* is a light-hearted reference to the fact that Macedonia was once inhabited by a medley of people . . .

300 g/11 oz carrots	**Serves 4**	½ lemon
300 g/11 oz baby turnips		1 tablespoon olive oil
225 g/8 oz green beans		freshly ground black pepper
400 g/14 oz baby peas (or 225 g/8 oz frozen *petits pois*)		150 ml/¼ pint/⅔ cup light mayonnaise (see page 13)
225 g/8 oz new potatoes		a few sprigs of fresh parsley, tarragon, chives and chervil
sea salt		

BRING A LARGE SAUCEPAN OF WATER TO the boil and start preparing the vegetables. Peel the carrots and baby turnips, then dice into small 0.5 cm/¼ in cubes. Top and tail the beans, then slice them into small 0.5 cm/¼ in segments. Shell the peas, then scrape and dice the new potatoes.

Add 2 teaspoons of salt to the boiling water. Throw in the carrots and turnips and bring back to the boil. Add the beans, peas and potatoes. If using frozen *petits pois*, don't add them until the water has come back to the boil the second time. Boil for a further 5–10 minutes, or until all the vegetables are cooked but not too soft. Drain well and transfer to a dish. Squeeze the lemon and sprinkle over the juice and olive oil, then season lightly with a little salt and freshly ground black pepper.

Leave until cold, then gently stir in the mayonnaise and snip over the fresh herbs. This dish will keep in the refrigerator for a day or two.

CHOU EN SALADE
Shredded Cabbage Salad

THIS WAS A favourite salad starter when I was a schoolgirl, ravenous but worried about my weight. I used to wolf down platefuls of the blissful stuff. The rest of the family was more discreet, but healthy, filling and economical *chou en salade* duly appeared at lunch-time once a week. To this day I prefer it to more complex coleslaw variations. The secret lies in the shredding (long, thin strips of cabbage imbibe the vinaigrette dressing better than short stubby pieces) and in the time spent marinating.

1 small white cabbage
1 tablespoon white wine
vinegar

Serves 4

90 ml/3 fl oz/⅓ cup groundnut
or olive oil
sea salt
freshly ground black pepper

DISCARD ANY BLEMISHED OUTER LEAVES. Cut the cabbage into 8 wedges and remove the core with a sharp knife. Rinse in cold water, shake well, then pat dry with absorbent paper or a clean tea-towel. Using a sharp and trusted knife, carefully shred the cabbage into fine strips, discarding any large ribs. Alternatively, use the shredding disc of a food processor.

Transfer the shredded cabbage to a salad bowl and stir in the vinegar. Pour in the oil, stir to coat, then season to taste with salt and freshly ground black pepper. Chill for a couple of hours, giving the salad a good stir once or twice.

Check the dressing before serving and add a little salt, pepper or oil as necessary. The salad tastes best generously coated with a strong dressing.

CAROTTES RÂPÉES
Grated Carrot Salad

MY FAVOURITE WAY to ingest this vitamin-laden vegetable. Grated carrots can be a little dry, hence the generous coating of oil and the soaking-in time.

400 g/14 oz carrots
1–2 lemons
1 hard-boiled egg
120 g/4 oz black olives

Serves 4

90 ml/3 fl oz/⅓ cup olive oil
sea salt
freshly ground black pepper
a few sprigs of fresh parsley

PEEL AND GRATE THE CARROTS. TRANSFER to a salad bowl. Squeeze the lemon (or lemons, if small) add the strained juice and toss the carrots to coat well. Grate in the hard-boiled egg, then stir in the black olives. Add the olive oil, toss well, then season lightly with salt and freshly ground black pepper. Refrigerate for at least 1 hour.

Remove from the refrigerator 20 minutes or so before serving. Check the seasoning and add a little extra oil, salt or pepper if necessary. Snip and stir in the parsley at the last minute.

ŒUFS BROUILLÉS PLM / *Scrambled Eggs PLM*

ŒUFS GRATINÉS
Gratin of Eggs and Gruyère

ŒUFS BROUILLÉS À LA TOURANGELLE
Scrambled Eggs with Rillettes

ŒUFS EN MEURETTE / *Eggs in Red Wine*

OMELETTE AUX FINES HERBES
Herb Omelette

PIPERADE
Tomato and Sweet Pepper Omelette

SOUFFLÉ AU GRUYÈRE / *Cheese Soufflé*

ESCARGOTS AU RIESLING
Snails with Wine Sauce

CROÛTES AU FROMAGE
Hot Cheese Croustades

CROQUE-MONSIEUR MAISON
Toasted Cheese and Ham

FEUILLETÉ AU ROQUEFORT
Roquefort Cheese Puff

GOUGÈRE / *Cheese Choux Ring*

PETITES BOUCHÉES / *Savoury Puffs*

TARTE À L'OIGNON / *Onion Tart*

PISSALADIÈRE
Provençal Onion and Anchovy Tart

QUICHE LORRAINE / *Quiche Lorraine*

TARTE À LA MOUTARDE
Mustard Tart

TARTE À LA RATATOUILLE
Mixed Vegetable Tart

TARTE AUX EPINARDS / *Spinach Tart*

CRÊPES FARCIES AUX EPINARDS
Pancakes Stuffed with Spinach

JAMBON À LA CRÈME
Ham in Cream and Port Sauce

Entrées Chaudes

Hot Starters

L ET ME BE frank about this. Several of the recipes in this chapter are at least as fiddly and time-consuming to prepare as main fish or meat courses. Don't let this put you off. There are a number of delectable old-fashioned classics waiting to make a come-back in the next 20-odd pages, from *tarte à l'oignon* to *gougère*, *escargots au Riesling* to *crêpes farcies*.

The solution is to regard them rather as the French are doing, increasingly often nowadays – as starters for special occasions or as *plats uniques*, low on fish and meat but perfectly satisfying in every other respect, when things are more casual and meals one or two courses shorter.

I think of these *entrées chaudes* as hot (or warm) snacks, some grander than others, of course, but all very relaxed, *très sympathiques*, and maybe a little tentative. The French don't really have a word for snack. The nearest to it is *casse-croûte*, which literally means to break the crust. *Entrées chaudes* are more elaborate, but they do break the edge of your appetite. You tend to eat them while you are hungry. Perhaps this is why they are so enjoyable: the best dish may yet be to come, during this meal or some future, more structured occasion, but who cares just now . . .

Œufs Brouillés PLM
Scrambled Eggs *PLM*

THE FIRST DISH my father taught me to cook and a perennial family treat. When in doubt, we had scrambled eggs for supper. Sometimes this was pure comfort food to cheer ourselves up in a still cold house after the drive from Paris. The cupboards may have been empty, but we never arrived without a dozen eggs, a salad and some bread. Herbs were usually to be found in the garden – however puny – and the *beurre salé* kept well in the fridge from one visit to the next. I write in the past tense but the scrambled eggs tradition continues. When PLM (my father's initials) is in charge of the menu he often gives them to his guests as a starter.

6 large eggs at room temperature	Serves 2–3	sprigs of fresh herbs – tarragon, chives, parsley, chervil, as liked
sea salt		1 tablespoon *crème fraîche* (optional)
freshly ground black pepper		
butter		toast or crusty bread, to serve

IN A BOWL, WHISK 5 EGGS BRISKLY, BUT without letting them become fluffy. Season lightly with salt and freshly ground black pepper. Melt a good knob of butter in a heavy-based saucepan over a very gentle heat. Tilt the pan to coat its sides with butter.

Pour in the eggs and cook gently, stirring very frequently with a wooden spoon and keeping the heat very low – this is not a dish you can abandon to have a chat on the phone, but you can snip the fresh herbs finely whilst keeping an eye on the egg mixture.

When the eggs begin to look set and cooked, add the remaining egg. Stir it in well, remove from the heat and add the snipped herbs, with, if you like, a little *crème fraîche* and extra butter. Serve at once, with toast or crusty bread. Refrain from eating your own helping until you have immersed the pan in very hot water – this will save a lot of effort later.

Œufs Gratinés
Gratin of Eggs and Gruyère

A CREAMY HOT egg starter which slips down a treat.

butter	Serves 4	90 ml/3 fl oz/⅓ cup double cream
150 g/5 oz Gruyère or strong mature Cheddar		sea salt
4 large eggs		freshly ground black pepper

HEAT THE OVEN TO 170°C/325°F/GAS 3. Generously butter a medium-sized gratin dish or 4 small individual dishes. Grate the cheese, then spread a good layer over the base of the dish or dishes, reserving about one-third for the topping. Carefully break the eggs over the grated cheese. Spoon 1 tablespoon of cream over each egg, and season well with salt and freshly ground black pepper. Sprinkle the remaining grated cheese over the eggs and cream. Dot with butter and cook in the oven for about 15 minutes, until golden. Serve very hot.

Œufs Brouillés à la Tourangelle
Scrambled Eggs with Rillettes

RILLETTES ARE A speciality of Touraine. They are made from pieces of pork, or goose, slowly cooked in fat in a large cauldron until molten to a soft fatty pâté – definitely a bit of an acquired taste, but detours are made by addicts of *rillettes* to find a *charcutier* who prepares them properly. They are a traditional local starter or snack, served with chunks of bread and a glass of cool Vouvray. Packed in little waxed carton pots, they will keep chilled for up to three weeks – well worth bringing back from France if you become addicted. They are particularly good combined with scrambled egg. And so are salmon *rillettes*, a satisfying combination of fresh and smoked salmon, spices, lemon juice and butter, not from Touraine, but now making an appearance on delicatessen counters all over this country.

90 g/3 oz *rillettes* of duck, pork, salmon or tuna	Serves 2–3	1 tablespoon *crème fraîche*
6 large eggs		a few sprigs of parsley
freshly ground black pepper		toast, to serve

MELT HALF THE *RILLETTES* IN A heavy-based saucepan over a very low heat. Tilt the pan around until its sides are coated with fat.

In a bowl whisk 5 of the eggs and season the mixture generously with freshly ground black pepper – the *rillettes* are fairly salty so there is no need to add salt.

Pour the eggs into the pan and cook patiently, keeping the heat low and stirring frequently with a wooden spoon, until they are almost set. Stir in the remaining egg and *rillettes*, then the *crème fraîche*. Remove from the heat. Snip a little parsley over the scrambled eggs and serve at once, with hot toast handed round separately.

Œufs en Meurette
Eggs in Red Wine

The Burgundy way of poaching eggs – in a strong red wine sauce. Keeping poached eggs warm is a little fiddly, so I have opted for the easier option of poaching the eggs at the last minute in simmering water with a few drops of vinegar rather than in the red wine stock.

Serves 4

4 large eggs

4 slices French bread

red wine vinegar

For the sauce

2 shallots

1 small onion

2 cloves of garlic

at least ½ bottle full-bodied red wine

1 sprig of thyme

1 bay leaf

1 sprig of parsley or chervil

90 g/3 oz/6 tablespoons butter, plus extra to finish the sauce

1 tablespoon flour

sea salt

freshly ground black pepper

Prepare the sauce. Peel and halve the shallots, onion and garlic (reserving half a clove). Make up the red wine to 750 ml/1¼ pints/scant 3¼ cups with water. In a saucepan, bring to the boil the wine and water, shallots, onion, garlic, thyme, bay leaf and parsley or chervil. Boil until reduced by half.

Meanwhile, mash together 60 g/2 oz/4 tablespoons butter and the flour and divide the paste into 4 small pieces. Strain the hot wine stock through a sieve into a smaller saucepan and gradually add the butter and flour paste, whisking in the pieces one by one. Whisking all the time, simmer the sauce for 2 minutes until thickened. Season to taste with salt and freshly ground black pepper. Keep hot, stirring occasionally.

Rub the bread with the cut side of the remaining garlic and fry in a little butter until golden brown on both sides. Keep warm.

Rinse out the first saucepan, pour in at least 1.7 l/3 pints/7½ cups boiling water, add a trickle of red wine vinegar, bring back to the boil, stir until the water swirls round, then lower the heat a little and carefully poach the eggs for 1–2 minutes. I find it easier to use a ladle to lower the eggs into the simmering water, and a slotted spoon to lift them out. Drain the eggs well on an impeccably clean folded tea-towel. Trim with scissors if they look too messy, then arrange one egg on each of the slices of fried bread. Whisk a few small knobs of butter into the sauce to make it look glossy, spoon it over the eggs and serve.

OMELETTE AUX FINES HERBES
Herb Omelette

This is one of the first recipes I remember watching someone cook, one of the first I wrote down, and, to my shame twenty years later, one that I still can't report to have constant success with. My mentor, Madame Boucher, used to manage 16 eggs at the same time in an incredibly heavy, battered black frying-pan. Invariably her omelettes turned out moistly creamy inside, packed with specks of fragrant herbs from the garden, and golden on the outside. Accompanied by that other deceptively simple dish, *Pommes de terre sautées* (see page 124), another Boucher triumph, it made a perfect dinner.

several sprigs of fresh herbs –
tarragon or chives, and parsley
and/or chervil

4 large eggs

1 tablespoon milk

Serves 2

sea salt

freshly ground black pepper

45 g/1½ oz/3 tablespoons
butter

Snip the herbs very finely and reserve. In a bowl, using a fork, beat the eggs briskly with one tablespoon cold water and the milk for about 20 seconds. Whisk in half the snipped herbs and season to taste with salt and freshly ground black pepper.

Meanwhile, heat a smallish heavy-based frying-pan until very hot. Add 30 g/1 oz/ 2 tablespoons butter and swirl it around to coat the pan. Before the butter starts browning, pour in the beaten eggs. Cook the omelette, shaking the pan to prevent the eggs sticking, and stirring the edges of the mixture towards the centre when it begins to set.

As soon as the eggs are no longer liquid but still looking moist, sprinkle half the remaining herbs over the omelette. Gently tilt the handle of the pan down towards you and fold the omelette back towards the centre with the help of a palette knife. Now lift up the handle of the pan away from you and turn the omelette upside down on to a heated plate. Trail the remaining butter over the omelette, sprinkle over the rest of the *fines herbes* and serve.

Piperade
Tomato and Sweet Pepper Omelette

My success rate with large folded omelettes being more than erratic, I have long been a fan of *piperade*, the celebrated sweet pepper and egg dish from the Basque country. It looks appetising, requires no folding and is a good dish to serve when you haven't got a great deal of time at the finish. Prepare the vegetable purée ahead and reheat while you are whisking the eggs. Serve with Bayonne ham, bread and a green salad for an easy supper or brunch.

	Serves 4	
1 large red pepper		2 slices Bayonne or other similar raw ham
1 onion		a little sweet vermouth or 1 teaspoon sugar
olive oil or bacon fat		
3 cloves of garlic		sea salt
3–4 ripe tomatoes		freshly ground black pepper
a pinch of dried thyme		8 large eggs
1 bay leaf		

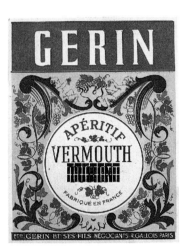

Wash and dry the pepper, then cut in half and remove the seeds, core and membrane. Char under the grill, uncut side up, until the skin is blistered. When the pepper is cool enough to handle, remove the skin and cut the flesh into small strips.

While the pepper is under the grill, chop the onion. In a large sauté pan or frying-pan, heat a little olive oil or bacon fat, and cook the onion with the whole garlic cloves, keeping the heat low. Blanch the tomatoes, then remove the skins and seeds and chop up the flesh. Add the tomatoes and pepper pieces, the thyme and bay leaf to the onion and continue to cook for about 15 minutes, stirring occasionally, until you have a thickish purée.

Chop the ham into pieces and add to the purée, with a sprinkling of sweet vermouth or 1 teaspoon of sugar to take away any acidity.

Season to taste with salt and freshly ground black pepper. Remove the garlic cloves and bay leaf. A few minutes before serving, reheat the pepper mixture.

Break 4 eggs into each of two bowls and beat briskly with a fork. Divide the pepper mixture between the two bowls and combine well with the beaten eggs. Generously grease two medium-sized frying-pans with olive oil and heat both pans and the grill. When the pans are hot, pour in the mixture, and cook for a few minutes over a low to medium heat, stirring frequently, until the bottom of the *piperade* is set.

Finish off under the grill for a couple of minutes, until lightly set and just coloured. I find it easier to produce a moist *piperade* using two smaller frying-pans, but you may prefer to cook it in a single batch. Serve at once.

Soufflé au Gruyère
Cheese Soufflé

Not exactly an original dish, I know, but one that is hard to beat and never fails to bring pleasure to the palate. I sometimes replace the Gruyère with 100 g/4 oz each of cooked ham and mushrooms, plus a shallot, all finely chopped. Proceed as below, but first sweat the chopped mushrooms and shallot in a little butter. Also use 90 ml/3 fl oz/⅓ cup dry white wine mixed with 150 ml/¼ pint/⅔ cup milk rather than plain milk when making the soufflé sauce.

250 ml/8 fl oz/1 cup milk

1 bay leaf

sea salt

freshly ground black pepper

90 g/3 oz/6 tablespoons butter, plus extra for greasing

75 g/2½ oz/½ cup flour

Serves 4–6

5 eggs

1 teaspoon strong Dijon mustard

grated nutmeg

120 g/4 oz Gruyère or other strong hard cheese

Bring the milk to the boil with the bay leaf, a pinch of salt and a little black pepper. Take off the heat. Melt the butter, add the flour and cook gently for a couple of minutes, stirring constantly with a whisk. Pour in the hot milk, whisking briskly and bring to the boil. Reduce the heat and simmer until the sauce is smooth and thick, stirring frequently. Remove from the heat.

Separate the eggs, then whisk the yolks into the sauce. Season with a little salt and pepper, the mustard and a pinch of nutmeg. Grate in the Gruyère. The mixture can be set aside for a while at this stage.

Heat the oven to 190°C/375°F/Gas 5. Generously butter a 20 cm/8 in soufflé dish. Whisk the egg whites until stiff. Using a large metal spoon, gently fold a little whisked egg white into the sauce. Fold in the rest thoroughly, working lightly and upwards, to keep in as much air as possible. Pour into the prepared soufflé dish, level with a spatula and bake for 25–35 minutes, until brown and well risen. Serve at once.

Escargots au Riesling
Snails with Wine Sauce

A very good way of serving snails if you don't happen to have the necessary equipment to extract them from their shells. You can, of course, start from scratch, with live snails, in which case this is a real plan-ahead recipe, as you have to starve them for a week before you start cooking . . . I know I am too feeble-hearted to last the course and likely to let the snails loose in the dead of night, so I use good quality canned *escargots* in this country and freshly cooked ones from the *charcutier* in France.

If you are disappointed not to see a proper snail butter recipe at this stage, turn to *moules farcies* (page 63) or *champignons farcis* (page 130). I love *beurre d'escargot*, best of all with mushrooms and second best with mussels, but somehow not with snails.

Serves 4

2 shallots

2 cloves of garlic

a small bunch of fresh parsley

60 g/2 oz/4 tablespoons butter, plus extra for the toast

24–30 snails, canned and drained, or freshly cooked

8 slices French bread

100 ml/3½ fl oz/generous ⅓ cup Alsace Riesling

2 teaspoons flour

120 ml/4 fl oz/½ cup *crème fraîche*

sea salt

freshly ground black pepper

Finely chop the shallots, 1 clove of garlic and the parsley. Melt the butter in a sauté pan. Add the chopped shallots and garlic and half the parsley. Stir for a few minutes over a gentle heat. Add the snails and sauté for 2–3 minutes, stirring occasionally.

Meanwhile, prepare the toast. Cut the remaining clove of garlic in half. Rub the bread with the cut sides of the garlic, then butter lightly. Heat the grill.

Pour the wine into the snail mixture and bring to a simmer. Sprinkle over the flour, stir and cook for 5–10 minutes. Stir in the *crème fraîche* and heat through gently. Toast the bread under the grill.

Season the snails generously with sea salt and freshly ground black pepper.

As a finishing touch, sprinkle over the remaining parsley and serve at once with the hot toast.

CROÛTES AU FROMAGE
Hot Cheese Croustades

A DISH I well remember circulating with at parties in my role of eldest daughter and *jeune fille de la maison*. French country bread, *pain de campagne*, was what we used. Monsieur Poilane's bread is ideal if you are lucky enough to be able to find it. Granary or any good dense-textured bread is a nice alternative. Don't dismiss the snipped chives as a mere garnish – they certainly look pretty but they also enhance the taste of the cheese topping. Try serving with a mixed leaf salad as a change from the ubiquitous goat's cheese starter.

	Serves 4	
6 slices Granary bread, medium cut		2 tablespoons *crème fraîche* or soured cream
60 g/2 oz/4 tablespoons butter		grated nutmeg
200 g/7 oz Gruyère or similar strongly flavoured hard cheese		freshly ground black pepper
2 small eggs		a few sprigs of chives

HEAT THE GRILL. IF YOU PREFER, REMOVE the crusts from the bread. Butter on one side. The slices can be left whole, halved or quartered – the smaller the better if you are serving them as finger food.

Grate the cheese into a bowl and mix with the eggs and cream. Season to taste with nutmeg and freshly ground black pepper. Generously spread the cheese mixture over the bread. Arrange in a heatproof dish and grill for a few minutes until golden brown.

Meanwhile finely snip the chives. Serve hot or *tiède*, sprinkled with snipped chives and a little extra black pepper.

CROQUE-MONSIEUR MAISON
Toasted Cheese and Ham

WHEN IN DOUBT, when you can't face the thought of cooking and can't think of anything to cook anyway, give them a *croque-monsieur*. Always in great demand from junior members of the family and not exactly frowned on by their seniors, the archetypal French café snack is wonderful emergency food.

	Serves 4	
3 tablespoons olive oil		4 thick slices good cooked ham off the bone
8 slices of bread		2–3 teaspoons Dijon mustard
60–90 g/2–3 oz/4–6 tablespoons butter	120 g/4 oz Gruyère or Cheddar	a few sprigs of chives

HEAT THE GRILL. IN A LARGE FRYING-pan, heat the olive oil and brown one side of each slice of bread. Remove from the pan, and butter the uncooked side of each slice, then grate the cheese and spread over 4 of the slices, on the buttered side. Heat under the grill until golden and melting.

Meanwhile divide the ham between the remaining buttered pieces of bread, trimming the ham slices to fit if necessary. Spread some mustard over the ham. Snip the chives and sprinkle them over the ham.

Melt the remaining butter in the frying-pan. Heat the ham-covered slices of bread in the hot butter, fried sides down.

Sandwich with the toasted cheese slices, cheese side down. Press well together and eat very hot.

FEUILLETÉ AU ROQUEFORT
Roquefort Cheese Puff

A MORE PROPER name for this recipe would be *demi-feuilleté au Roquefort*, since the pastry is very much a short cut on traditional puff. The filling is rich and festive.

FOR THE PASTRY

225 g/8 oz/1½ cups flour

pinch of salt

90 ml/3 fl oz/⅓ cup double cream

120 g/4 oz/8 tablespoons butter, plus extra for greasing

1 egg yolk and a little milk, for glazing

Serves 6–8

FOR THE FILLING

4 eggs

150 g/5 oz Roquefort

90 g/3 oz/⅓ cup cream cheese

90 ml/3 fl oz/⅓ cup single cream

freshly ground black pepper

a small bunch of fresh chives

TO MAKE THE PASTRY BY HAND, SIFT THE flour and salt into a bowl. Make a well and add the cream. Lightly work the flour into the cream, adding a couple of tablespoons of very cold water if the flour isn't completely absorbed. Cut the butter into very small pieces, add half to the flour and knead gently until absorbed, working the pastry as little as possible. Divide the pastry into 4, mix a bit of butter into each piece, then roll together to form a large ball.

If you are using a food processor, cut the butter into very small pieces. Briefly process the flour and salt. Add half the butter and process until the mixture resembles bread-crumbs. With the machine still running, add the cream and one tablespoon of very cold water until the dough starts to form a ball and comes off the sides of the bowl. Add the remaining butter, dotting evenly over the dough, and process just long enough to mix it well in.

Whichever method you have used, once you have a ball of dough, turn it out on to a floured board, then flatten lightly with a floured rolling pin and fold and roll a couple of times. Chill the folded pastry for at least half an hour (but no longer than 1 hour otherwise it hardens too much) before using.

Meanwhile, prepare the filling. Whisk the 4 eggs. In another bowl, mash the Roquefort with a fork. Combine the Roquefort, cream cheese and cream, whisking the mixture until fairly smooth. Add the eggs and whisk well. Season generously with freshly ground black pepper and snip in the chives.

Heat the oven to 190°C/375°F/Gas 5. Separate the pastry into two pieces, with one 'half' slightly larger than the other. Roll out into circles. Grease a large flan tin and spread the smaller pastry circle on it. Prick well with a fork. Spoon the filling over the pastry.

Cover with the remaining pastry. Insert a pastry funnel in the centre to allow the steam to escape. Press the edges lightly together with dampened fingers to seal the top and bottom layers. Score the top in a diamond pattern with a knife. Glaze the pastry with beaten egg yolk and a little milk. Bake for 40–45 minutes.

GOUGÈRE
Cheese Choux Ring

As satisfying to make as to eat, particularly with a good glass of wine. This recipe is for a *gougère* ring. To make individual puffs, keep the paste balls at least 2.5 cm/1 in apart when you pipe or spoon them on to the baking tray.

120 g/4 oz/8 tablespoons butter, plus extra for greasing	Serves 6	3–4 eggs
150 g/5 oz/1 cup flour		120 g/4 oz Emmental, Comté or mature farmhouse Cheddar
250 ml/8 fl oz/1 cup water		freshly ground black pepper
salt		dash of milk, for glazing

BEURRE NATUREL "DU PRÉ FLEURI"

·68·Bᵈ ANSPACH. BRUX. Tel. 276,00

Cut the butter into dice. Sift the flour on to a sheet of greaseproof paper. In a heavy-based saucepan, bring the water, diced butter and a pinch of salt to the boil. The minute the liquid begins to boil, remove the pan from the heat. Quickly and all at once add the flour and immediately start stirring it in with a spatula or wooden spoon. Return to the heat and continue to stir briskly until the paste leaves the sides of the pan and looks smooth and a little shiny.

Remove from the heat and stir for 1 minute. Add the eggs one at a time, mixing them in vigorously until the paste comes together again. Beat the last egg before you add it in, since you may need only a fraction of it: you should end up with a glossy, floppy paste, not a runny, liquid one. Continue beating for another minute or so to give the paste more body. Cut the cheese into slivers and beat into the paste. Season with freshly ground black pepper.

Heat the oven to 190°C/375°F/Gas 5. Grease a baking tray. Fit a piping bag with a plain 1 cm/½ in nozzle and spoon the paste into the bag. Pipe a large ring of small balls of paste on the baking tray, keeping them no further than 2 cm/¾ in apart. If you don't like using a piping bag, you can use a tablespoon – the final effect will not be quite so tidy but no matter. Brush the paste lightly with any remaining egg yolk mixed with a splash of milk.

Bake for about 30 minutes, until well risen and golden. Turn the oven off (and open the door if electric). Leave the *gougère* to stand for 5 minutes before taking it out. Serve hot or warm.

PETITES BOUCHÉES
Savoury Puffs

A *BOUCHÉE* IS a mouthful, and I have always thought of these soft-centred little morsels as excellent 'mouth-fillers'. They certainly give the hostess or host time to control the subject of the conversation while guests are palatably occupied . . .

If you are getting out your piping bag to make neat choux puffs, try piping some of the paste into small éclairs for contrast. These *bouchées* are good cold, but don't assemble them more than 1–2 hours ahead. Unfilled baked puffs or éclairs will freeze well, otherwise use on the day you make them.

FOR THE CHOUX PUFFS

120 g/4 oz/8 tablespoons butter, plus extra for greasing

150 g/5 oz/1 cup flour

250 ml/8 fl oz/1 cup water

salt

3–4 eggs

freshly ground black pepper

300 ml/½ pint/1¼ cups thick béchamel (see page 13)

FOR THE PRAWN FILLING

90 g/3 oz cooked peeled prawns

Serves 6

2 tablespoons double cream

cayenne pepper

a few sprigs of chives

FOR THE MUSHROOM FILLING

30 g/1 oz/2 tablespoons butter

175 g/6 oz brown cap mushrooms

1 clove of garlic

2 teaspoons tomato purée

a few sprigs of parsley

FOR THE BLUE CHEESE FILLING

90 g/3 oz Fourme d'Ambert or similar blue cheese

1 stick of celery

2 tablespoons double cream

paprika

HEAT THE OVEN TO 190°C/375°F/GAS 5. Make the choux paste (see page 51) and pipe or spoon on to a greased baking tray, keeping the paste balls at least 2.5 cm/1 in apart. Bake for about 30 minutes, until well risen and golden. Leave to cool a little.

Meanwhile prepare the fillings. To make the prawn filling, press the prawns dry between 2 sheets of absorbent paper, then cut in half. In a bowl, mix together one-third of the béchamel, the chopped prawns and the cream. Season with a good pinch of cayenne and a little salt. Snip in the chives.

To make the mushroom filling, melt the butter in a small frying-pan. Finely chop the mushrooms and garlic, then sauté over a moderate heat. In a bowl, combine one-third of the béchamel with the tomato purée. Stir in the sautéed mushrooms and snip in the parsley. Season with a little salt and black pepper.

Now make the blue cheese filling. Mash the cheese with a fork. Finely chop the celery. Mix with the remaining béchamel and the cream. Season with a good pinch of paprika.

Slit the puffs with a knife. Spoon the prawn filling into one-third of the puffs, the mushroom filling into another third and the blue cheese filling into the rest.

Tarte à l'Oignon
Onion Tart

A VERY ONIONY onion tart. The evaporated milk adds a distinctive rich sweetness to the filling.
If you like a touch of *lardons* with onions, try adding to the filling about 90 g/3 oz chopped and sautéed
smoked streaky bacon.

Serves 8

FOR THE PASTRY

150 g/5 oz/10 tablespoons cold butter, plus extra for greasing

225 g/8 oz/1½ cups flour

1 pinch of salt

1 teaspoon sugar

1 egg

1 egg white

FOR THE FILLING

1.2 kg/2½ lbs large white onions

2–3 fresh sage leaves

4–5 tablespoons olive oil

3 eggs

100 ml/3½ fl oz/generous ⅓ cup evaporated milk or single cream

30 g/1 oz strong Gruyère or similar cheese

sea salt

freshly ground black pepper

grated nutmeg

PREPARE THE PASTRY CASE. CUT THE butter into small pieces. If you are using a food processor, quickly process together the flour, salt and sugar, then add the butter and process until the mixture looks like breadcrumbs. Add the egg and 5 or 6 tablespoons of cold water. Process until the mixture comes off the sides of the bowl. Remove from the bowl, work lightly with your hands into a ball and chill for at least 30 minutes – and up to 24 hours if this is convenient.

Alternatively, cut up the butter and leave to soften. Sift the flour into a bowl with the salt and sugar. Make a well, add the pieces of butter, the egg and 5 or 6 tablespoons of cold water. Mix with your fingertips without trying to get a smooth paste. Add a little more water if necessary – the paste should be supple but not soft. Form into a ball and chill as above.

Butter a large loose-bottomed tart tin. Roll out the pastry, then spread it into the greased tin, using your hands to press it in lightly without stretching it. Prick with a fork and chill for 10 minutes to allow it to relax.

Heat the oven to 200°C/400°F/Gas 6. Line

the pastry shell with greaseproof paper or foil and fill with dried beans. Bake for 15–20 minutes. Meanwhile prepare the filling. Very thinly slice the onions – it doesn't matter if the slices break. Finely snip the sage leaves. In a large frying-pan, heat the olive oil, then gently sweat the onion slices with the chopped sage until soft and blond, but not too browned. Keep the heat very low and the pan covered, occasionally lifting the lid to stir the onions. Allow a good 30 minutes for the onions to be really soft.

Remove the dried beans and lining paper from the pastry case. If the base still feels very soft, return the tin to the oven for a few minutes. Leave to cool a little, then brush the pastry with a little egg white. Turn the oven down to 190°C/375 °F/Gas 5.

Lightly whisk together the eggs and the evaporated milk or cream. Stir into the onion mixture. Grate in the cheese. Season generously with salt and freshly ground black pepper, and a little nutmeg. Pour into the prepared pastry case and bake for 15–20 minutes. Serve warm rather than hot.

PISSALADIÈRE
Provençal Onion and Anchovy Tart

A FAVOURITE SUMMER dish and one that I have always thought of as 'convenience' food, because we always used fresh bread dough from the village baker for the base. Had I been more romantic I would perhaps have been reminded of the days of communal baking . . .

Now that I cannot easily get hold of fresh bread dough I use bought puff pastry, frozen or fresh, and concentrate on gently cooking the filling until the onions sweetly melt. The tomatoes do not feature in original Provençal recipes for *pissaladière* but I like their texture.

450 g/1 lb ready-made puff pastry	Serves 6–8	sea salt
butter or oil, for greasing		freshly ground black pepper
1 small egg, separated	4 tablespoons strong olive oil	1 teaspoon sugar
FOR THE FILLING	2 tomatoes	about 24 canned anchovy fillets
1 kg/2¼ lbs large white onions	a few sprigs of fresh thyme	about 12 black olives

PREPARE THE FILLING. THINLY SLICE THE onions. Heat the oil in a large frying-pan and sauté the onions over a very low heat. Meanwhile, blanch, peel, seed and chop the tomatoes. Add to the onions with the sprigs of thyme, and continue to sauté over a low heat for 30 minutes, until the onions are very soft. Stir occasionally and watch that the onions don't brown.

Heat the oven to 220°C/425°F/Gas 7. Roll out the pastry to about 0.5 cm/¼ in thick. Grease a baking sheet. Cut the pastry into a 25 cm/10 in square and spread on the baking sheet.

Cut the remaining pastry into 4 strips, 25 cm/10 in long and 1 cm/½ in wide. Brush the surface of each strip with a little egg white,

then stick one strip along each side of the pastry square, brushed surface down.

Remove the sprigs of thyme from the frying-pan. Season the onion and tomato filling very lightly with salt and pepper and stir in the sugar. Spoon the filling as evenly as possible over the pastry, keeping clear of the edges. Drain the anchovy fillets. Arrange attractively over the filling and dot about the black olives.

Beat the remaining egg white with the yolk and brush the edges of the pastry. Bake for 15–20 minutes, then lower the heat to 190°C/375°F/Gas 5 and bake for a further 5–10 minutes, until the top is golden and the pastry base cooked – check by lifting it a little with a palette knife. Eat *tiède* or at room temperature rather than hot.

QUICHE LORRAINE
Quiche Lorraine

CLOSE YOUR EYES and think of ten classic French dishes. I would be surprised if *quiche lorraine* did not feature somewhere on your list. You may be surprised to hear that this most famous French dish, the matriarch of the egg-and-cream-filled family of tarts, derives its name from that very German word for cake – *Kuchen*. The original *quiche lorraine* recipes from Nancy did not include cheese, but many people prefer it with, so I have added it as an optional extra. More important than the presence, or absence, of cheese is the quality of the bacon you use. The best bet (and a bit of a tall order) is traditional cure lightly-smoked streaky bacon, cut into very thick rashers.

225 g/8 oz/16 tablespoons cold butter, plus extra for greasing

375 g/13 oz/2½ cups flour

pinch of salt

FOR THE FILLING

225 g/8 oz smoked streaky bacon, cut into very thick rashers

Serves 6–8

1–2 tablespoons olive oil

3 large eggs

150 ml/¼ pint/⅔ cup double cream or *crème fraîche*

freshly ground black pepper

sea salt, if you like

30 g/1 oz/2 tablespoons butter

45 g/1½ oz Gruyère (optional)

PREPARE THE PASTRY CASE. CUT THE butter into small cubes. If you are using a food processor, quickly whizz together the flour and salt. Add half the butter, and process until the mixture looks like breadcrumbs. With the machine still running, add 5 or 6 tablespoons of cold water through the feed tube and process until the mixture forms a ball and comes off the sides of the bowl. Divide the ball into 4, return to the processor and add the remaining butter (dotted evenly over the dough). Process until well mixed.

Remove the dough from the bowl. On a floured board, roll it into a long rectangle, (you don't need to be too pedantic about this – rounded corners are fine) and then fold both ends towards the centre. Roll out again and repeat 3 times. Chill for at least 30 minutes.

Alternatively, sift the flour and salt into a bowl. Make a well, add 5 or 6 tablespoons of very cold water, and lightly gather the flour into the water.

Work the dough with your fingertips, then flatten it on a floured board. Dot with the cubes of cold butter, press them in well and fold over 3 times crossways, like a letter, then 3 times lengthways. Chill for 10 minutes and then roll and fold as above 3 more times, leaving the

dough to rest in the refrigerator in between the rollings.

Heat the oven to 190°C/375°F/Gas 5. Butter a large loose-bottomed tart tin. Roll out the pastry, then spread it into the greased tin, using your hands to press it in lightly. Allow it to overhang a little from the tin. Prick all over with a fork.

Line the pastry case with foil or greaseproof paper and fill with dried beans. Bake for 15–20 minutes, then remove the beans and lining paper. Meanwhile make the filling. Remove the rind from the bacon, then cut into 0.75 cm /⅓ in pieces. If you suspect that the bacon is very salty, blanch it in boiling water and pat it thoroughly dry with absorbent paper. Heat the oil and sauté the bacon until golden. Drain on absorbent paper. Spread the bacon evenly over the pastry and press in a little.

Beat the eggs and the cream, season generously with freshly ground black pepper and, if you like, a very little salt (don't forget, the bacon is already salty). Pour into the pastry case and dot with butter. If you are using Gruyère, grate it and sprinkle over the tart before adding the butter. Bake for 15–20 minutes, until set. Cover the tart with greaseproof paper if it is colouring too quickly. Serve warm.

TARTE À LA MOUTARDE
Mustard Tart

A ROBUST TART for mustard lovers.

1 pastry case, half-baked (see *tarte à l'oignon* on page 53)

FOR THE FILLING

150 g/5 oz Gruyère or similar strong cheese

2 tablespoons strong Dijon mustard

Serves 6–8

2 tablespoons single cream or evaporated milk

3 tomatoes

sea salt

freshly ground black pepper

dried thyme and savoury

2 tablespoons strong olive oil

PREPARE AND BAKE THE PASTRY CASE. TURN the oven to 190°C/375°F/Gas 5. Make the filling. Grate the cheese and sprinkle one quarter of it over the pastry base. Mix the mustard with the cream or evaporated milk and pour over the grated cheese.

Blanch and peel the tomatoes. Cut into thin slices and remove the seeds. Sprinkle another quarter of the cheese over the mustard/cream mixture. Arrange the tomato slices on top. Season lightly with salt and pepper. Crumble in a pinch or two of dried herbs and cover with the remaining cheese. Sprinkle on the olive oil and add a further seasoning of black pepper, if so desired.

Bake for about 20 minutes, until golden brown. Leave to cool slightly before serving and eat *tiède*.

TARTE À LA RATATOUILLE
Mixed Vegetable Tart

A MOST DEPENDABLE COMBINATION and a civilised way of using leftover ratatouille (see the recipe on page 126). If you are starting from scratch, halve the quantities given in the recipe and leave out the parsley and final tablespoon of olive oil. If you have not got quite enough ratatouille left, simply slice 2 or 3 small courgettes, sauté them lightly and quickly in a very little olive oil, then stir them into the mixture. Better still, if you happen to come upon one or two perfect large ripe tomatoes, just seed and chop them straight into your ratatouille. No need to peel them first. Serve, like other savoury tarts, as a starter (for 6–8) or with a salad as a relaxed main course (for 4–6).

1 pastry case, fully baked (see page 53)

cooked ratatouille (see above)

Serves 6–8

1 or 2 ripe tomatoes (see above)

PREPARE AND BAKE THE PASTRY CASE. TURN the oven to 190°C/375°F/Gas 5.

Chop and seed the tomatoes, then stir them into the ratatouille. Spoon the mixture into the prepared pastry case and smooth flat. Bake the tart for 10–15 minutes, then remove from the oven and leave to cool until barely warm before serving.

Tarte aux Epinards
Spinach Tart

Like many of its fellow savoury tarts, *tarte aux épinards* is a very easy dinner party first course, as it is best eaten barely warm and can be dealt with before the guests arrive. It would be dishonest of me not to mention that I sometimes make this dish with 450 g/1 lb frozen spinach, well drained, instead of the fresh stuff when speed is of the essence – or the market spinach-less.

1 pastry-case, half-baked (see *tarte à l'oignon* recipe on page 53)

FOR THE FILLING

1.5 kg/3 lbs fresh spinach

sea salt

75 g/2½ oz/5 tablespoons butter

1 tablespoon flour

Serves 6–8

250 ml/8 fl oz/1 cup *crème fraîche*

freshly ground black pepper

4 eggs

grated nutmeg

25 g/1 oz Gruyère or similar strong cheese

Prepare and bake the pastry case. Make the filling while the pastry case is in the oven. Trim and wash the spinach. Wilt the leaves for 1 minute in a little salted boiling water. Drain well in a colander, pushing with a wooden spoon to extract as much moisture as possible. Chop roughly. Melt a knob of butter in a pan, add the chopped spinach and sweat for 2 minutes. Reserve.

In a saucepan, melt the remaining butter. Add the flour and cook for 2 minutes, stirring constantly. Spoon in the *crème fraîche* and cook until thickened, stirring frequently. Season generously with salt and freshly ground black pepper. Remove from the heat.

Beat the eggs thoroughly, then whisk into the cream sauce. Fold three-quarters of this mixture into the spinach. Check the seasoning and add a little nutmeg. Pour into the half-baked pastry case. Top with the remaining cream and egg sauce. Grate the cheese and sprinkle over the tart.

Bake on 190°C/375°F/Gas 5 for about 20 minutes, until firm and golden. Leave to cool before serving – this tart tastes better *tiède* than hot.

CRÊPES FARCIES AUX ÉPINARDS
Pancakes Stuffed with Spinach

BRING BACK OLD-FASHIONED savoury crêpes! They are fun to make, good-natured enough to keep overnight and they take kindly to leftovers. The rather beery batter below was adapted *en famille* a long time ago from a totally beery Raymond Oliver recipe which had only a little milk to melt the butter in. Vary the blend to suit your taste – there are no hard and fast rules.

The ham, shallot and mushroom mixture I suggested as a soufflé alternative (see page 47) works well as a pancake filling. So does a little left-over cold chicken, briefly sautéed with snipped tarragon leaves, then stirred into the béchamel. Add a little double cream and leave out the Gruyère.

---

175 g/6 oz/generous 1 cup flour

sea salt

3 eggs

60 g/2 oz/4 tablespoons butter, plus extra for the filling and to finish

about 175 ml/6 fl oz/¾ cup milk

about 175 ml/6 fl oz/¾ cup beer

oil for greasing

Makes about 15 pancakes

FOR THE FILLING

450 g/1 lb/2¼ cups cooked and drained spinach, or 1.5 kg/3 lbs fresh spinach

350 ml/12 fl oz/1½ cups thick béchamel (see page 13)

120 g/4 oz Gruyère

sea salt

freshly ground black pepper

grated nutmeg

SIFT THE FLOUR AND SALT INTO A BOWL. Make a well. Beat the eggs as for an omelette and melt the butter with a little of the milk. Using a small hand-whisk, gently stir together the flour and eggs, then gradually pour in the milk and beer. Stir lightly until the batter is smooth and just thick enough to coat your finger. Add the melted butter and stir a little longer. Strain through a fine sieve or *chinois* and preferably leave to stand for a couple of hours.

To cook the pancakes, very lightly grease a smooth heavy-based frying-pan. I use a wad of absorbent paper dipped in a little oil. Heat the pan until very hot and ladle in just enough batter to cover the bottom thinly – tip the pan to spread it evenly. Cook over a medium-high heat until the underside is golden. Turn over with a palette knife and cook the other side. The first pancake sometimes sticks a little, but it tends to become easier as it gets going. If your first pancake looks a little dry, whisk a little more melted butter into the batter. If it is thin and tears easily, sift in a little flour and whisk in briskly. Re-grease the pan if necessary. Allow 2–3 minutes for each pancake. Once cooked, stack on a plate and cover with tin foil until ready to use. This is a good time to take a break: the pancakes will keep overnight in the refrigerator.

Heat the oven to 200°C/400°F/Gas 6. Prepare the filling. If using fresh spinach, trim, rinse and blanch in boiling water. Drain well in a colander, pressing hard to get rid of excess moisture. Chop finely. Sweat the chopped spinach in a little butter. Stir into the béchamel. Grate the Gruyère and stir half into the spinach sauce. Season with a little salt, a generous amount of black pepper and a good pinch of nutmeg.

Butter a baking dish. Spoon some filling over each pancake. Roll up and place in the dish. Sprinkle the pancakes with the remaining Gruyère, dot with butter and bake for 10–15 minutes, until hot and golden brown. Serve at once.

Jambon à la Crème
Ham in Cream and Port Sauce

WHEN I MOVED into my first flat after leaving university, my aunt Yonnée – who is a nice combination of intellectual, *gourmande* and good cook – empathised with my situation. What could a novice cook and fledgling career-girl impress her friends with? She gave me as a culinary bible her own copy of Curnonsky. She looked through her cards, books and scrapbooks and went to a great deal of trouble to write down her chosen recipes. I was quite overwhelmed, but this quick and easy starter soon caught my eye. It works well, followed by a large *salade niçoise*, as a quick supper – particularly if your guests turn up the minute you walked in.

4 thick slices of good cooked ham off the bone

30 g/1 oz/2 tablespoons butter

mini croissants, to serve

Serves 4

FOR THE SAUCE

90 ml/3 fl oz/⅓ cup port

90 ml/3 fl oz/⅓ cup tomato *coulis* (see page 15)

90 ml/3 fl oz/⅓ cup soured cream or *crème fraîche*

sea salt

freshly ground black pepper

Jambons.Saucissons.Salaisons.Conserves.
"ALHAMBRA"

HEAT THE OVEN TO 100°C/200°F/GAS LOW. Heat the croissants and the serving dish. Make the sauce. In a saucepan combine the port, tomato *coulis* and cream. Heat this mixture until very hot but be careful not to boil. Stir frequently.

Meanwhile, melt the butter in a frying-pan and quickly heat the ham. Roll each slice and place in the heated serving dish. Season the sauce with a little salt and plenty of ground black pepper. Pour over the rolled ham. Serve at once with the warm croissants.

MOULES MARINIERE/*Mussels in White Wine*

MOULES FARCIES/*Stuffed Mussels*

SALADE DE MOULES AUX POMMES DE TERRE
Mussels with Potato Salad

SOUPE DE MOULES/*Mussel Soup*

COQUILLES SAINT-JACQUES À LA CRÈME ET AU SAFRAN
Scallops with Saffron Cream

COQUILLES SAINT-JACQUES AU BEURRE BLANC
Scallops with Shallot Butter

COQUILLES SAINT-JACQUES SURPRISE
Scallops with a Puff Pastry Lid

LANGOUSTINES/*Scampi*

SOUPE DE POISSONS MADAME BASTIER
A Provençal Fish Soup

COLIN POÉLÉ SAUCE MOUTARDE
Pan-fried Cod with Mustard Sauce

COLIN POÉLÉ PETITE SAUCE MOUTARDE
Cod Steaks with Quick-Mustard Sauce

RAIE AU BEURRE NOIR/*Skate in Black Butter*

LOTTE À LA PROVENÇALE
Monkfish with Tomato and Herbs

GRATIN DE HADDOCK AU RIZ
Gratin of Smoked Haddock

BRANDADE DE MORUE/*Purée of Salt Cod*

MORUE PARMENTIER/*Salt Cod with Potatoes*

MORUE EN AÏOLI
Salt Cod with Garlic Mayonnaise

FILETS DE MERLAN AUX PETITS LÉGUMES
Baked Whiting Fillets with Vegetables

TRUITE AUX PIGNONS/*Trout with Pine Nuts*

TRUITE AUX CHAMPIGNONS
Trout with Mushrooms

DAURADE FARCIE AUX AMANDES
Sea Bream with Almond Stuffing

TERRINE DE POISSONS ANNE-SOPHIE
Sole and Salmon Terrine

PAIN DE POISSON DE TOUS LES JOURS
Family Fish Loaf

PAIN DE POISSON POUR INVITÉS
Posh Fish Loaf

POISSONS ET FRUITS DE MER

FISH AND SEAFOOD

OUR LOCAL STREET market, rue Poncelet in the XVIIth, wasn't particularly distinguished by Paris standards. Naturally it was noisy, narrow and colourful. It was also unpretentiously very well supplied. I still pay it my respects whenever I am staying in Paris. Its glorious fish and seafood displays – and choice – I still miss a great deal. Finding good seafood or fish in London is an expensive and laborious exercise, reeking of foodie snobbery.

It seems that Paris was always well supplied with fish. When Elizabeth of Austria, the new wife of King Charles IX, first arrived in Paris in 1570, the municipality decided to hold a banquet in her honour. But it was Lent and the Church kept to its rules. No meat was to be allowed. The Queen Mother's fishmongers came to the rescue. No problem. They could guarantee to supply sole, turbot, mullet, trout, carp, pike, lamprey, salmon (fresh and salted), shad, herring, lobsters, crabs, crayfish, mussels and a thousand frogs. They couldn't quite promise mackerel, sturgeon, porpoise and tortoise, but they were hopeful . . . Not a bad spread to pick from.

Moules Marinière
Mussels in White Wine

A HOME-GROWN COMPROMISE: this version of *moules marinière* includes a little cream, but is not as rich as the roux-and-egg based *moules poulette*.

2.3 l or 1.8 kg/4 pints or 4 lbs mussels in their shells

2 shallots

1 clove of garlic

60 g/2 oz/4 tablespoons butter

several sprigs of parsley

Serves 4–6

a few sprigs of chives

a few sprigs of thyme

250 ml/8 fl oz/1 cup dry white wine

200 ml/7 fl oz/generous ¾ cup water

sea salt

freshly ground black pepper

½ lemon

60 ml/2 fl oz/¼ cup double cream

fresh crusty bread, to serve

SCRUB THE MUSSELS UNDER RUNNING water and remove the black beards. Discard any mussels that remain open or look cracked. Keep the mussels in plenty of cold water.

Finely chop the shallots and garlic. Melt the butter in a very large saucepan, then add the chopped shallots and garlic. Sweat for a couple of minutes, then snip in the parsley, chives and thyme, reserving a few sprigs to finish the dish. Pour in the white wine and water and bring to the boil. Reduce the heat and simmer the liquid for a few minutes.

Add the mussels, turn up the heat and season with very little salt and plenty of black pepper. Cook for a few minutes, until the mussels open, shaking the pan occasionally. Squeeze in the lemon juice. If any mussels have failed to open, discard them. Remove the mussels with a slotted spoon and heap in a large bowl.

Increase the heat a little, add the cream to the pan and stir in well. Pour the sauce over the mussels. Snip over the rest of the fresh herbs and serve at once with plenty of fresh crusty bread.

MOULES FARCIES
Stuffed Mussels

A GLORIOUS DISH. I like my stuffed mussels exceedingly garlicky, but the flavoured butter will still be
delicious even if you go very easy on the garlic.

2.3 l or 1.8 kg/4 pints or 4 lbs
large fat mussels in their shells

1 large onion

1 carrot

100 ml/3½ fl oz/generous ⅓
cup dry white wine

1 bay leaf

Serves 4–6

a few sprigs each of parsley
and thyme

freshly ground black pepper

fresh crusty bread, to serve

FOR THE STUFFING

2–4 cloves of garlic

several sprigs of parsley

several sprigs of chives

150 g/5 oz/10 tablespoons
butter, softened

60 g/2 oz/1 cup breadcrumbs,
made from slightly stale bread

sea salt

freshly ground black pepper

SCRUB THE MUSSELS WELL WITH A HARD
brush under plenty of cold running water and
pull off the black beards. Discard any cracked
mussels and any that are still open at this stage.
Keep the mussels in a large bowl of cold water.

Chop up the onion and carrot. Pour the wine
into a very large saucepan. Add the onion,
carrot, bay leaf, parsley and thyme, then season
with a little pepper.

Throw in the mussels and cook over a high
heat for a few minutes until the shells open,
shaking the pan occasionally. Remove the
mussels from the pan with a slotted spoon and
discard any that are still closed. As soon as they
are cool enough to handle, remove the mussels

from their shells. Reserve the mussels and the
bottom shells.

Heat the oven to 230°C/450°F/Gas 8. Now
make the stuffing. Finely chop the garlic. Snip
the parsley and chives very finely. Using a
fork, mash together the soft butter, garlic,
parsley, chives and breadcrumbs. Season with a
little salt and plenty of black pepper.

Using a teaspoon or the point of a small
knife, put a little flavoured butter in each
half-shell. Add a mussel, then cover with a
good layer of flavoured butter. Arrange the
mussels in a single layer in a large gratin dish.
Bake for 8–10 minutes, until sizzling brown.
Serve immediately with fresh crusty bread.

SALADE DE MOULES AUX POMMES DE TERRE
Mussels with Potato Salad

A SUBSTANTIAL BUT very happy combination of mussels, potatoes and mayonnaise.

3–4 large waxy potatoes

sea salt

90 ml/3 fl oz/⅓ cup olive oil

1½ tablespoons white or red wine vinegar

2 teaspoons mustard

freshly ground black pepper

2.3 l or 1.8 kg/4 pints or 4 lbs mussels in their shells

Serves 6

1 large onion

1 carrot

100 ml/3½ fl oz/generous ⅓ cup dry white wine

several sprigs of parsley

a few sprigs of thyme

150 ml/¼ pint/⅔ cup mild mayonnaise (see page 13)

several sprigs of chives

MAKE THE POTATO SALAD. BRING THE potatoes to the boil in plenty of lightly salted water. Reduce the heat and simmer gently until the potatoes are cooked but still firm. Drain the potatoes and leave to cool in a colander until you can handle them comfortably. Remove the skin and cut the potatoes into medium-thick slices.

Whisk together the olive oil, vinegar and mustard. Season liberally with salt and black pepper. Distribute the dressing over the potatoes, and gently turn them over until evenly coated.

Prepare and cook the mussels as described for *moules farcies* (page 63). Lift the mussels out of the cooking liquid with a slotted spoon. Stir 1–2 tablespoons of the cooking liquid into the mayonnaise, a little at a time. Remove the mussels from their shells and discard the shells. Leave to cool. Once the mussels are cold, toss them in the mayonnaise and season with freshly ground black pepper.

Heap the mussels in the centre of a round dish. Surround with the potato salad. Chop the parsley and chives and sprinkle over the potato salad. Serve at room temperature.

Soupe de Moules
Mussel Soup

My mother's recipe for mussel soup, full of fragrance. Both mussels and soup can be cooked several hours ahead and assembled at the last minute.

Serves 6

2.3 l or 1.8 kg/4 pints or 4 lbs mussels in their shells

1 large onion

2 carrots

600 ml/1 pint/2½ cups dry white wine

1 bay leaf

a bunch of parsley

a few sprigs of thyme

freshly ground black pepper

2 leeks

2 shallots

30 g/1 oz/2 tablespoons butter

750 ml/1¼ pints/scant 3 cups water

1 clove of garlic

6 chunky slices of French bread

olive oil for sprinkling

120 ml/4 fl oz/½ cup single cream

1 large egg yolk

sea salt

Prepare and cook the mussels as described for *moules farcies* (page 63). Strain and reserve the cooking liquid. Remove the mussels from their shells as soon as they are cool enough to handle. Discard the shells.

Finely chop the remaining carrot, the leeks and the shallots. Melt the butter in a large saucepan and gently sweat the chopped vegetables without letting them brown. After a few minutes, pour in the remaining 500 ml/16 fl oz /2 cups white wine, the water and the reserved cooking liquid. Bring to a simmer and cook for a few minutes.

Heat the grill. In a small bowl snip the rest of the parsley. Cut the garlic in half and rub the bread with the cut sides of garlic. Sprinkle with olive oil and toast lightly on both sides under the grill.

Add the mussels to the liquid with half the parsley. Return to a simmer. Combine the cream and the egg yolk with 1 tablespoon of the hot liquid. Stir the mixture into the soup. Check the seasoning. This soup needs plenty of fresh ground black pepper. Sprinkle with the remaining parsley and serve at once with the hot garlic toast.

COQUILLES SAINT-JACQUES À LA CRÈME ET AU SAFRAN
Scallops with Saffron Cream

THIS DISH IS more of a main course than the other scallop recipes. Serve with long-grain rice cooked in a light stock.

12–16 scallops, off their shells

a few sprigs of parsley

2 tablespoons brandy

1 tablespoon olive oil

30 g/1 oz/2 tablespoons butter

Serves 4

a pinch of powdered saffron

200 ml/7 fl oz soured cream

1 egg yolk

sea salt

cayenne

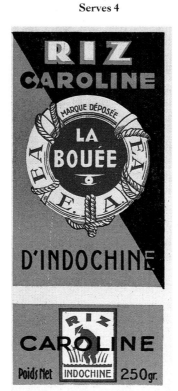

RINSE THE SCALLOPS UNDER COLD RUNNING water. Remove any gristle and black threads. Separate the orange coral from the white flesh, and cut the flesh into 2–3 discs, depending on the size of the scallops. Snip the parsley into a small bowl. Put the prepared scallops in a soup plate. Sprinkle with brandy, cover and marinate for at least 30 minutes, turning the scallops over once or twice.

Heat the oil and butter in a sauté pan. Drain the scallops and collect the brandy juices. Reserve the corals. Gently cook the slices of scallop flesh with three-quarters of the parsley in the hot oil and butter, for 2–3 minutes, just long enough for the scallops to change colour and become firmer. Turn the scallops over once

or twice during cooking. Remove them from the pan with a fish slice and set aside.

Now mash half the corals in a small bowl. Stir the saffron into the hot fat, then add the mashed corals, the cream and the brandy. Bring to the boil and simmer for a couple of minutes, stirring frequently, then add the rest of the corals and cook for another minute.

Beat the egg yolk with two tablespoons of the hot saffron cream. Stir into the pan and reduce the heat – the mixture should no longer be allowed to boil. Continue stirring for a minute or so, then add the reserved scallop slices. Heat through, season lightly with salt and cayenne, then sprinkle with the rest of the parsley and serve.

COQUILLES SAINT-JACQUES AU BEURRE BLANC
Scallops with Shallot Butter

A CLASSIC WAY of preparing scallops, and one of my favourites. The only problem is that this recipe does require constant attention. You can make the *court bouillon* and reduce the shallots well in advance, but after that, allow a totally uninterrupted quarter of an hour at the stove. The sauce will keep warm for a few minutes over hot water, but the scallops will cool quickly . . .

Serves 4

8–12 scallops, off their shells

1 onion

4 shallots

250 ml/8 fl oz/1 cup dry white wine

300 ml/½ pint/1¼ cups water

bouquet garni

sea salt

freshly ground black pepper

60 ml/4 tablespoon/¼ cup white wine vinegar

200 g/7 oz/14 tablespoons butter

a few sprigs of parsley and chives (optional)

MAKE A LIGHT *COURT BOUILLON*. CHOP the onion and one of the shallots, and bring to the boil in a sauté pan with the white wine, water and bouquet garni. Season and simmer for 10 minutes. Strain the liquid into a bowl, discard the onion, shallot and bouquet garni, and return to the pan.

Start preparing the shallot butter sauce. Very finely chop the rest of the shallots. Cook, with the vinegar, in a small saucepan until soft and syrupy – this will take a good 15 minutes. Cut the butter into small pieces.

Rinse the scallops under cold running water, remove any gristle and black threads. Separate the orange coral from the white flesh and cut the flesh into 2–3 discs, depending on the size of the scallops. Add the scallops, the white flesh first, the corals after 1 minute, to the simmering liquid and cook very gently for a few

minutes – again this will depend on size, usually from 2–5 minutes. If the scallops aren't entirely covered by the liquid, add extra water, very hot but not boiling. Do not allow to boil and be careful not to overcook, since this will toughen the flesh and damage the corals. Reserve 3 tablespoons of the cooking liquid. Drain the scallops and keep warm.

Meanwhile, carry on cooking the sauce. Whisk the butter into the shallot purée, a few pieces at a time, without ever letting the mixture come to the boil. Whisk briskly and continuously, occasionally taking the pan off the heat. Trickle the reserved cooking liquid, a little at a time, into the finished sauce, whisking well. Check the seasoning. Snip a few sprigs of parsley and chives into the sauce, if you like, and spoon the sauce over the scallops just before serving.

COQUILLES SAINT-JACQUES SURPRISE
Scallops with a Puff Pastry Lid

I CANNOT REMEMBER exactly where I first ate this dish. All I remember is that it was a long time ago, in someone's house and with my parents . . . I like serving seafood first courses in scallop shells and the puff pastry lids are fun to break into.
The method also works well with folded fillets of sole or turbot, perhaps with the addition of a small pinch of saffron.

8–12 scallops, and 4 large, undamaged, saucer-shaped scallop shells

1 shallot

200 g/7 oz button mushrooms

1 tablespoon olive oil

Serves 4

4 tablespoons dry white wine

several sprigs of chives

30 g/1 oz/2 tablespoons butter

sea salt

cayenne pepper

a little flour

350 g/12 oz ready-made puff pastry (thaw if frozen)

1 egg yolk

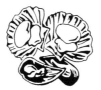

RINSE THE SCALLOPS WELL UNDER COLD running water. Remove the greyish gristle around the cushion and the black threads, then separate the coral from the white flesh and cut the flesh into 2–3 discs, depending on the size of the scallops. Wash the scallop shells, scrubbing them if necessary. Dry well.

Steam the prepared scallops for 2–3 minutes over boiling water. Meanwhile, finely chop the shallot. Wipe the mushrooms and slice very thinly. Heat the oil and soften the shallot and mushrooms for a couple of minutes over a low heat. Put a baking tray in the oven and heat to 220°C/425°F/Gas 7.

Divide the shallot and mushroom mixture between the prepared shells. Cover with slices of scallop and coral. Moisten with the white wine. Snip in some chives. Add a small knob of butter and season lightly with salt and cayenne.

On a lightly floured board, roll out the pastry very thinly. Cut into 4 circles, slightly larger than the scallop shells. Place a pastry 'lid' over each filled scallop shell. Score the pastry attractively with a sharp knife. Make a hole in the centre to allow the steam to escape. Now seal the pastry. Press the edges down all the way round with moistened fingers, then brush the edges with a little egg yolk.

Bake for 1 minute, then remove from the oven and brush all over the pastry lids lightly with egg yolk to glaze. Bake for a further 10 minutes. Serve immediately.

LANGOUSTINES
Scampi

TRULY A FOOD to feast on. *Langoustines* traditionally feature on the family menu at least once sometime over Christmas and the New Year. Since every other French family tends to do just the same, and prices inevitably rocket a little higher every year, this isn't a particularly bright move in terms of economics. Even apart from Christmas, *langoustines* have always been a family treat. When one member of the family wants to be nice to us all, he or she buys as many crustaceans as the cash flow permits, makes a mayonnaise, and we tuck merrily in – armed with a bottle of Chablis or Alsace Pinot Gris, finger bowls, large napkins and suitable hardware to extract the last bit of flesh from the claws. Not a pretty sight for outsiders but plenty of happy memories for the Moines.

There are elaborate ways of cooking *langoustines*, but not in my book. I think they are best either *au naturel* or simply pan-fried. Allow 6 *langoustines* per person, 4 at the very least. The heads and shells are worth keeping for making stock.

24 raw, unshelled *langoustines*	Serves 4	LANGOUSTINES POÊLÉES:
LANGOUSTINES AU NATUREL:		1 tablespoon olive oil
150 ml/¼ pint/⅔ cup dry white wine	90 g/3 oz/6 tablespoons butter, if serving hot	60 g/2 oz/4 tablespoons butter
sea salt	150 ml/¼ pint/⅔ cup mayonnaise (page 13), if serving cold	1 shallot
2 shallots		1 clove of garlic
1 bay leaf	1 lemon	several sprigs of parsley
		1½ lemons

LANGOUSTINES AU NATUREL

IN A VERY LARGE SAUCEPAN, BRING TO THE boil plenty of water, the wine, a generous pinch of salt, the shallots and bay leaf. Simmer for a few minutes.

Wash the *langoustines* in cold water. Turn up the heat, bring the liquid back to a fast boil and add the *langoustines*. Return to the boil and cook for 5 minutes.

Turn off the heat and leave the *langoustines* in the stock for a few minutes. Drain, refresh under cold water and serve either hot with melted butter, or cold with mayonnaise. Serve both variations with wedges of lemon.

LANGOUSTINES POÊLÉES

TO PAN-FRY THE *LANGOUSTINES*, COOK THEM as before for 2 minutes only. As soon as they are cool enough to handle, shell them. Start by twisting, or cutting, off the heads. Pull the shell apart, slitting the undersides with scissors if necessary, then holding the tail shell and pulling the meat free. Remove any large dark intestinal threads, rinse and dry.

Heat the oil and butter in a large sauté pan. Chop the shallot and garlic and soften for a minute. Add the *langoustines* and sauté gently all over for 2–3 minutes. Snip in the parsley and sprinkle with the juice of ½ lemon. Serve with pan juices, and with lemon wedges.

Soupe de Poissons Madame Bastier
A Provençal Fish Soup

Cherchez le poisson – it's not easy to get *rascasse*, *girelles* and *sarans* away from the Mediterranean shores. I use a mixture of red mullet, brill, smoked cod (for its strong flavour), large prawns and crab flesh. An extra pinch of saffron will help if you feel your ingredients are too bland.

about 1.5 kg/3 lbs fish, cleaned, gutted, and chopped, and shellfish	Serves 4	2 sprigs of rosemary
		sea salt
2 large white onions		freshly ground black pepper
3 cloves of garlic		To serve
1 bulb of fennel	2–3 tablespoons olive oil	pieces of toast rubbed with garlic (see recipe for *soupe de moules* page 65)
1–2 potatoes	½ teaspoon of ground saffron	
2 large ripe tomatoes	a bunch of thyme	*rouille* (page 36)

Prepare the vegetables. Chop the onions, garlic and fennel. Peel and slice the potatoes. Blanch, peel, seed and chop the tomatoes.

In a heavy-based flameproof casserole or large saucepan, heat the oil and gently sauté the onions, garlic and fennel until very lightly browned. Stir in the fish and cook for a few minutes, then add about 1.2 1/2 pints/5 cups water, the potatoes, saffron, thyme, rosemary and tomatoes. Bring to the boil, then reduce the heat and simmer for 20–25 minutes, until the potatoes are cooked.

Now comes the slightly messy bit of the recipe. Remove the fish and vegetable pieces from the casserole with a slotted spoon; pick out and discard as much skin, bones and sprigs of herbs as you can and pass the rest through a *mouli* – or whizz in a food processor. Return to the heat and finish cooking for 5–10 minutes. Season and serve with toast rubbed with garlic and *rouille*.

COLIN POÊLÉ SAUCE MOUTARDE
Pan-fried Cod with Mustard Sauce

FRIDAY WAS, AND still is, Fish Day in France. As good-ish Catholics we religiously had it, but my Protestant cousins on my father's side had it too and so did all my schoolfriends. Perhaps it was because the fishmongers' displays were always at their shimmery best on Fridays . . .

I used to beg for sole and *langoustines*. Too expensive, said my mother. Cod was much better value and it duly appeared on the table practically every Friday lunch-time. It was pan-fried, but alas not accompanied by mustard sauce. I only liked the 'burnt bits' and considered the dish to be the height of boring family food. It took me years, and a nice down-to-earth fishmonger's stall in my local Portobello Road market, to enjoy cod. Pity this reliable fish had by then become so expensive.

The mustard sauce is a personal favourite, evolved from a recipe my mother was very fond of. I use it with all kinds of fish, poached, grilled or pan-fried, and it is pretty good with white meat too.

	Serves 4	
4 cod steaks		250 ml/8 fl oz/1 cup double cream
1 tablespoon flour	FOR THE MUSTARD SAUCE	1–1½ tablespoons Dijon mustard
sea salt	2 shallots	
cayenne pepper	1 small bunch of flat-leafed parsley	sea salt
dried thyme		freshly ground black pepper
1 tablespoon olive oil	60 g/2 oz/4 tablespoons butter	1 egg yolk
30 g/1 oz/2 tablespoons butter	1 tablespoon flour	½ lemon

DRY THE COD STEAKS WELL WITH ABSORbent paper. Season the flour with a little salt, cayenne pepper and a pinch of dried thyme.

Prepare the mustard sauce. Finely chop the shallots and snip the parsley. Heat half the butter in a small heavy-based saucepan. Sweat the shallots and parsley in the melted butter over a low heat, making sure neither butter nor shallots change colour. Stir in the rest of the butter, then sprinkle in the flour as soon as it has melted. Cook for a couple of minutes, stirring briskly, then add the cream. Continue to cook until thick and smooth, then stir in the mustard. Taste and season well with salt and freshly ground black pepper.

Meanwhile, cook the fish. Heat the oil in a frying-pan large enough to take the cod steaks comfortably. Add the butter and once it has melted, add the fish. Pan-fry the cod for about 4 minutes on each side, depending on thickness, keeping the heat moderate. The fish tends to disintegrate if you cook it too fast or too long. Turn over carefully half way through with a fish slice.

Just before you are ready to serve, beat the egg yolk with the juice of the half lemon in a small bowl. Add 2 tablespoons of the sauce, beat until combined, then stir the mixture into the saucepan. If the sauce seems too thick at this stage, thin it down with a few teaspoons of boiling water, stirred in one at a time. Arrange the cod steaks on a serving dish. Spoon over some of the sauce and sprinkle with snipped parsley. Serve the rest of the sauce separately.

Colin Poêlé Petite Sauce Moutarde
Cod Steaks with Quick-Mustard Sauce

A QUICKIE VERSION of the previous recipe. More basic, certainly, but lighter and a good simple dish.

4 cod steaks	Serves 4	90 ml/3 fl oz/⅓ cup double cream
1 tablespoon flour		30 g/1 oz/2 tablespoons butter
sea salt	30 g/1 oz/2 tablespoons butter	2–3 teaspoons Dijon mustard
cayenne pepper	FOR THE QUICK-MUSTARD SAUCE	sea salt
dried thyme	90 ml/3 fl oz/⅓ cup dry white	freshly ground black pepper
1 tablespoon olive oil	wine	a few sprigs flat-leafed parsley

COOK THE FISH AS IN THE PREVIOUS recipe. Remove from the frying-pan with a fish slice and keep warm in the serving dish. Turn up the heat a little. Swirl the wine into the frying-pan, then whisk in the cream and continue stirring while the liquid reduces a little.

Cut the butter into small pieces. Stir the mustard into the sauce. Dot the butter pieces around the pan and stir until they are melted. Season quickly with salt and freshly ground black pepper. Pour or spoon the sauce over the fish and snip the parsley over the lot. Serve immediately.

Raie au Beurre Noir
Skate in Black Butter

As I AM only too aware, there is one slight problem with this justly famous dish: only a few seconds separate *beurre noir* from acrid *beurre brûlé* . . . Disaster is just around the corner. I can offer no remedy. The only thing you can do is tip the evil stuff out, pat the pan clean with a wad of absorbent paper and start again.

1 kg/2¼ lbs skate wings	Serves 4	freshly ground black pepper
90 ml/3 fl oz/⅓ cup red wine vinegar	1 small onion, quartered	several sprigs of parsley
a few sprigs of thyme	1 small carrot, quartered	120 g/4 oz/8 tablespoons butter
1 bay leaf	sea salt	3 tablespoons capers

POACH THE FISH. PLACE THE SKATE WINGS in a sauté pan large enough to take the wings comfortably. Cover with cold water, then add 2 tablespoons of vinegar, the thyme, bay leaf, onion and carrot. Season lightly with salt and freshly ground black pepper. Bring to the boil over a low heat, then simmer gently for 10–12 minutes, until the flesh is just tender enough to flake with a fork. Meanwhile, snip the parsley into a bowl and melt the butter over a very low heat. Remove the skate from the pan with a fish

slice. Drain, remove the skin if necessary, and pat the flesh dry with absorbent paper. Put the fish on a serving dish and sprinkle with the parsley. Reserve a little poaching liquid.

Turn up the heat under the butter just a little and swirl the butter until it turns golden brown. Trickle half of it over the skate and parsley. Return the pan to the heat, swirl in the rest of the vinegar, the capers and a couple of tablespoons of poaching liquid. Stir until heated through, pour over the fish and serve.

Lotte à la Provençale
Monkfish with Tomato and Herbs

THIS UNPRETENTIOUS DISH was definitely inspired by Provence, but I cannot guarantee that it is one hundred per cent authentic . . . Use plenty of fresh herbs and very ripe tomatoes.

800 g/1¾ lb monkfish, without skin and bones

1 large white Spanish onion

6 tablespoons olive oil

4 ripe tomatoes

2 cloves of garlic

Serves 4

a small bunch of parsley

a few sprigs of fresh thyme

a few sprigs of rosemary

sea salt

freshly ground black pepper

150 ml/¼ pint/⅔ cup dry white wine

60 g/2 oz Gruyère or mature farmhouse Cheddar

CUT THE FISH INTO 8–10 EVEN-SIZED pieces. Pat dry with absorbent paper. Finely chop the onion. Heat the oven to 180°C/350°F/Gas 4.

Heat half the oil in a large frying-pan. Briskly sauté the fish with half the chopped onion over a moderately high heat, turning the pieces over carefully. The monkfish will soon become firmer and golden white.

Coat a large ovenproof dish with the remaining oil. Remove the monkfish and onion from the frying-pan with a fish slice and put them in the baking dish. Blanch the tomatoes, then peel and slice them thinly. Discard the seeds. Arrange the tomato slices over the fish.

Finely chop the garlic. In a small bowl, snip the fresh herbs, reserving a few sprigs of parsley to finish off the dish. Add the rest of the onion and the garlic to the fresh herbs and stir well. Scatter the mixture over the fish and tomatoes. Season with salt and black pepper and pour in the wine. Grate the cheese over the dish.

Bake for 15–20 minutes until sizzling and golden brown. Snip the rest of the parsley over the dish and serve hot.

GRATIN DE HADDOCK AU RIZ
Gratin of Smoked Haddock

I STILL HAVE my mother's index card with her blueprint of this recipe, in her precise and elegant handwriting. She wasn't at all convinced when I told her I thought *gratin de haddock au riz* was rather like an Anglo-Indian classic called kedgeree . . . The basic ingredients may be similar, but the cheesy *gratin* method and the end result are definitely very French.

Serves 4

800 g/1¾ lbs skinned smoked haddock fillets

1.2 l/2 pints/5 cups milk

60 g/2 oz/4 tablespoons butter

grated nutmeg

1 egg

225 g/8 oz/1 cup long grain rice

sea salt

90 g/3 oz Gruyère or strong Cheddar

3 tablespoons breadcrumbs made with day-old bread

a small bunch of parsley

freshly ground black pepper

RINSE THE HADDOCK. IN A SAUCEPAN wide enough to take the haddock fillets side by side, bring the milk to a simmer with a knob of butter and a good pinch of nutmeg. Hard-boil, then shell the egg. Meanwhile, add the haddock to the milk and poach for 5–8 minutes, until firm and just cooked. Lift out of the pan with a slotted spoon, drain and set aside on absorbent paper. Reserve the milk in the pan.

Cook the rice in another saucepan for 3 minutes in lightly salted boiling water. Bring the milk back to the boil. Drain the rice and pour into the boiling milk. Reduce the heat a little and simmer for 15 minutes, or until the rice is cooked.

Heat the oven to 200°C/400°F/Gas 6. Butter an ovenproof dish. Drain, refresh and again drain the rice, then spread over the ovenproof dish. Pat dry with absorbent paper. Grate half the cheese over the rice. Shred the haddock, removing all the bones you can spot, and spread over the rice and grated cheese.

Grate the rest of the cheese over the haddock. Sprinkle with the breadcrumbs, then snip the parsley into a small bowl. Scatter most of the parsley over the dish, reserving a little to finish off. Dot with small pieces of butter. Season with black pepper and bake for 5–10 minutes, until crisp and golden brown.

Grate the hard-boiled egg into the bowl with the reserved parsley. Mix and sprinkle over the dish just before serving.

BRANDADE DE MORUE
Purée of Salt Cod

PERHAPS IT WAS because the village church wasn't heated but, as a child, I always found Good Friday a shivery experience. The happiness of Easter Sunday seemed an intolerably long way away. The warmest thing about Good Friday was *brandade de morue*, smooth, creamy, pleasingly fishy and very comforting. The recipe below is the one I prefer. When I cook *brandade* for my father who has a marked fondness for *crème fraîche* I use double the amount of cream to avoid complaints – and the irritating sight of a large undistinguished tub being ostentatiously passed around the table.

450 g/1 lb salt cod	**Serves 4–6**	4 tablespoons double cream
1 bouquet garni		freshly ground black pepper
3 cloves of garlic		garlic croûtons, to serve, if liked
200 ml/7 fl oz/generous ¾ cup olive oil	100 ml/3½ fl oz/generous ⅓ cup milk	butter to reheat, if wished

SOAK THE SALT COD FOR AT LEAST 12 HOURS in plenty of cold water, changing the water several times.

Break the fish into several chunks. Place in a sauté pan with the bouquet garni, cover with cold water, bring to the boil and simmer for 10 minutes. Remove from the pan, drain well. Discard the skin and as many bones as possible, and shred the salt cod very finely into a large bowl. While the fish is simmering, finely chop the garlic and gently heat the olive oil and milk in separate pans.

Put the bowl of shredded salt cod over a pan of simmering water. Gradually pour in half the warm olive oil, pounding the mixture well with a large pestle or wooden spoon. Work in the garlic, then the rest of the oil and the warm milk, a little at a time – this will take about 10 minutes and you should end up with a thick, slightly sticky, white purée.

Stir in the cream and season generously with freshly ground black pepper. Serve at once, if you like with garlic croûtons. Alternatively, leave to get cold. To reheat, butter a gratin dish, spoon the *brandade* into the dish, smooth the top and dot with butter. Reheat in the oven on 190°C/375°F/Gas 5 for 15 minutes or so before serving.

MORUE PARMENTIER
Salt Cod with Potatoes

THIS DISH REQUIRES less elbow grease than *brandade de morue*. Make sure you poach the cod very gently since it tends to toughen when boiled too fast or for too long.

Serves 4–6

450 g/1 lb salt cod

450 g/1 lb waxy potatoes

sea salt

1 bouquet garni

1 large white onion

1 tablespoon olive oil

200 ml/7 fl oz/generous ¾ cup béchamel (see page 13)

butter, for greasing, and to finish

cayenne pepper

45 g/1½ oz Gruyère or strong Cheddar, grated

several sprigs of parsley, chopped

freshly ground black pepper

SOAK THE SALT COD IN PLENTY OF COLD water for at least 12 hours, changing the water several times. Cook the potatoes in barely boiling, lightly salted water until just tender. Drain, refresh and peel the potatoes as soon as they are cool enough to handle. Cut them into thick slices.

While the potatoes are boiling, poach the salt cod. Break it into chunks. Place in a sauté pan with the bouquet garni, cover with cold water, bring to the boil, then simmer gently for 10 minutes. Drain well. Discard as much skin and bones as possible, then shred the cod.

Heat the oven to 200°C/400°F/Gas 6. Finely chop the onion. Heat the oil in a small frying-pan and sweat the onion over a low heat for a few minutes, stirring frequently. Remove from the pan with a slotted spoon, drain on absorbent paper, then stir the onion into the béchamel.

Butter a gratin dish. Spread the slices of potato over the dish. Cover with the shredded salt cod and season with a little cayenne pepper. Cover with the onion béchamel. Scatter the cheese and parsley over the béchamel. Season with freshly ground black pepper, dot with butter, and bake until golden brown. Serve hot.

Morue en Aïoli
Salt Cod with Garlic Mayonnaise

Vary the vegetables according to what is in season. Cooked beetroot is a popular accompaniment.

1 kg/2¼ lbs salt cod	Serves 6	several sprigs of thyme
4 eggs		2 bay leaves
8 small potatoes		1 onion
sea salt		150 ml/¼ pint/⅔ cup dry white wine
4 carrots		
3 bulbs of fennel		350 ml/12 fl oz/1½ cups garlic mayonnaise (see page 13)
1 small cauliflower		2 tomatoes
400 g/14 oz green beans		freshly ground black pepper

Soak the salt cod in plenty of cold water for at least 12 hours, changing the water several times.

Once the fish is de-salted, hard-boil the eggs and start preparing the vegetables. Scrub the potatoes, then cook them in lightly salted water. Peel the carrots, cut them into chunks and cook in lightly salted boiling water. Trim and halve the fennel bulbs and cook with the carrots. Cut the cauliflower into florets and cook in lightly salted water. Top and tail the beans and cook with the cauliflower florets. The vegetables should all be cooked through but not soft. Refresh them quickly under cold running water and drain well.

Now poach the fish. Break the cod into chunks. Place in a large sauté pan with the thyme, bay leaves, onion, and wine. Cover with cold water, bring to the boil, turn the heat down and simmer very gently for 12–15 minutes, until the fish is just tender. Remove the fish from the pan, drain well, refresh and drain again. Discard skin and bones and coarsely shred the fish. Beat 1–2 tablespoons of the poaching liquid into the garlic mayonnaise.

Arrange the shredded salt cold in the centre of a large serving dish. Shell the hard-boiled eggs and cut them in half lengthways. Quarter and seed the tomatoes. Arrange the tomatoes and eggs around the salt cod. Surround with the cooked vegetables.

To finish, season the dish with a little freshly ground black pepper and serve with the bowl of garlic mayonnaise.

FILETS DE MERLAN AUX PETITS LÉGUMES
Baked Whiting Fillets with Vegetables

Whiting may not be many people's favourite fish, but it responds very well to the treatment below. This is a good method for cooking all the humbler varieties of white fish.

Serves 4

6 whiting fillets, skinned

200 g/7 oz carrots

120 g/4 oz celery

200 g/7 oz brown cap mushrooms

2 shallots

45 g/1½ oz/3 tablespoons butter

sea salt

freshly ground black pepper

200 ml/7 fl oz/generous ¾ cup single cream

120 ml/4 fl oz/½ cup dry white wine

a few sprigs of chervil

a few sprigs of chives

Prepare the vegetables. Peel the carrots, and slice into small *julienne* matchsticks. Trim the celery and cut into narrow slices. Halve and finely slice the mushrooms. Finely chop the shallots.

In a sauté pan, melt half the butter and gently cook the carrots, celery and mushrooms over a low heat for about 10 minutes, stirring occasionally. Season with salt and black pepper and stir in half the cream. Cook, partly covered for 5 more minutes, still over a low heat. Do not allow to boil.

Heat the oven to 180°C/350°F/Gas 4. Spread the vegetables into a baking dish large enough to take the whiting in a single layer. Put the fillets on top of the vegetables. Sprinkle with the chopped shallots. Trickle the white wine and the rest of the cream over the fish. Season lightly with salt and more generously with black pepper. Dot with the remaining butter and bake for 15–20 minutes or until just cooked.

Snip the fresh herbs over the fish and serve hot.

TRUITE AUX PIGNONS
Trout with Pine Nuts

AN EASY VARIATION, which I particularly like, on the well-known theme of trout with almonds.

	Serves 4	
4 trout, cleaned and gutted		60 g/2 oz/scant ½ cup pine nuts
1 lemon	2 tablespoons olive oil	45 g/1½ oz/3 tablespoons
a few sprigs of thyme	sea salt	butter
a few sprigs of marjoram	freshly ground black pepper	3 tablespoons dry white wine

HEAT THE OVEN TO 190°C/375°F/GAS 5. Cut the lemon in half, then cut one half into 4 slices and squeeze the other half. Cut 4 pieces of foil large enough to comfortably envelop the trout.

Place a trout in the centre of each piece of foil. Put a little thyme and marjoram inside each trout, then sprinkle the cavity with a few drops of olive oil and season lightly with salt and freshly ground black pepper. Place a slice of lemon on each trout, sprinkle with a few pine nuts, a little olive oil and lemon juice.

Season lightly. Wrap the foil around the fish, and seal well. Bake for 15–20 minutes, until the flesh is just tender enough to flake.

Meanwhile, melt a knob of butter in a small frying-pan and sauté the rest of the pine nuts until golden. Remove them from the pan with a slotted spoon and drain on absorbent paper. Swirl the white wine into the pan. Add the rest of the butter and stir until melted. Open the foil parcels a little. Sprinkle in the fried pine nuts and trickle in a little wine and butter sauce. Serve immediately.

TRUITE AUX CHAMPIGNONS
Trout with Mushrooms

A RECIPE BORROWED from another happy French exile in London, Marie-France Sandon. I have often prepared trout in this pleasingly different way since first tasting it at Marie-France's.

	Serves 4	
4 trout, cleaned and gutted	several sprigs of parsley	sea salt
120 g/4 oz button mushrooms	2 bay leaves	freshly ground black pepper
4 shallots	200 ml/7 fl oz/generous ¾ cup	150 ml/¼ pint/⅔ cup single
several sprigs of fresh thyme	lager or light ale	cream

WIPE AND THINLY SLICE THE MUSHROOMS, then chop the shallots very finely. In a sauté pan large enough to take the trout in a single layer, spread the mushrooms and shallots. Add the thyme, parsley and bay leaves, reserving a few sprigs of parsley. Moisten with the beer and season lightly with salt and freshly ground black pepper. Bring to the boil, then lower the heat and simmer for about 10 minutes.

Add the fish to the pan, with just enough water to cover. Return to a simmer and poach

for 10 minutes over a gentle heat, until the fish is just tender enough to flake with a fork. Remove the trout from the pan with a fish slice. Drain well and put on a serving dish.

Turn up the heat and boil the poaching liquid until well reduced – to about half the original quantity. Discard the sprigs of herbs and the bay leaves. Stir in the cream until heated through. Pour the sauce over the fish. Snip the rest of the parsley over the dish, season again and serve immediately.

Daurade Farcie aux Amandes
Sea Bream with Almond Stuffing

WHAT A CONSUMER-FRIENDLY fish the sea bream is, with its firm flesh and untreacherous bones. This is a fun dish to make. The stuffing can be prepared well ahead and chilled, leaving only the little surgical job and the finishing touches to do before baking. The cooked fish will stay hot enough for a good 20 minutes in the oven if need be, but cut back on the cooking time a little.

Serves 4–6

1 sea bream weighing about 800 g/1¾ lbs

2 eggs

60 ml/4 tablespoons/¼ cup milk

1 thick slice of bread without the crust

1 large white Spanish onion

1 shallot

1 clove of garlic

3 tablespoons olive oil, plus extra if necessary

about 24 fresh shelled almonds

several sprigs of parsley

a few sprigs of thyme

a sprig of rosemary

1 bay leaf

sea salt

freshly ground black pepper

45 g/1½ oz/generous ½ cup breadcrumbs made with day-old bread

45 g/1½ oz/3 tablespoons butter

150 ml/¼ pint/⅔ cup dry white wine, plus extra if necessary

PREPARE THE STUFFING. HARD-BOIL AND shell 1 egg. Heat the milk to boiling point in a small saucepan and soak the bread until cool enough to handle. Drain and squeeze with your hands to get rid of the excess moisture. Combine the onion with the shallot and garlic in a food processor. Heat 1 tablespoon of olive oil and sauté the mixture for a few minutes over a low heat, stirring frequently.

Without rinsing the bowl of the food processor, whizz half the almonds until fine. Add the parsley, thyme, rosemary, bay leaf, hard-boiled egg and bread, whizz, then moisten with the remaining egg. Add the sautéed onion, season lightly with salt and black pepper and whizz again.

Heat the oven to 190°C/375°F/Gas 5. Slit the belly of the fish open with a sharp knife. Wipe the cavity with absorbent paper, then spoon in the stuffing. The stuffing will expand during cooking, so don't pack the cavity too tightly. Sew up the slit to secure the stuffing. Coat a large baking dish with 1 tablespoon of olive oil. Put the fish in the dish and spoon any remaining stuffing around it. Brush the fish with the rest of the oil, and sprinkle on the breadcrumbs. Cut the rest of the almonds into slivers, and scatter over the fish. Cut the butter into small pieces and dot all over. Moisten with the white wine.

Cover the dish with foil or greaseproof paper and bake for 40–50 minutes. Baste a few times with the cooking juices. If the dish looks too dry, add extra wine and a little more olive oil. After about 30 minutes, remove the foil or greaseproof paper to allow the topping to turn golden brown. Remove the thread and serve piping hot.

Terrine de Poissons Anne-Sophie
Sole and Salmon Terrine

Cold fish terrines make good first courses for large family reunions, when you want to serve something reasonably impressive but have precious little time at the last minute. My sister's handsome dish is a reliable favourite. You can process the herbs for the sauce a little ahead, but don't whisk it up until you are nearly ready to sit people down at the table.

	Serves 8–10	
45 g/1½ oz/3 tablespoons butter		2 tablespoons brandy
3 small sole, skinned and filleted		sea salt
750 g/1½ lbs salmon steaks, skinned and boned		freshly ground black pepper
oil for greasing		grated nutmeg
		chilli powder
12 large prawns in their shells, to finish the dish	450 g/1 lb whiting, skinned and boned	For the sauce
a few sprigs of parsley or watercress, to finish the dish	150 g/5 oz/10 tablespoons butter	a large bunch of watercress
For the stuffing	2 eggs	several sprigs each of parsley, chives and chervil
250 ml/8 fl oz/1 cup milk	12 egg yolks	300 ml/½ pint/1¼ cups *crème fraîche*
30 g/1 oz/scant ½ cup fresh white breadcrumbs	550 ml/18 fl oz/2⅓ cups double cream or *crème fraîche*	½ lemon
		freshly ground black pepper

Melt the butter in a large frying-pan and gently sauté the sole fillets and salmon steaks, a few at a time over a low heat. Leave to get cold. Meanwhile, prepare the stuffing. Bring the milk to the boil in a small saucepan, then stir in the breadcrumbs. Reduce the heat and let the mixture thicken a little, stirring it occasionally.

Chop the whiting finely in a food processor, then feed in the butter, eggs and yolks, and the milk mixture. Process until smooth. Tip or spoon the mixture into a large bowl. Whisk in the cream, a little at a time. Trickle in the brandy, still stirring. Season lightly with salt and more generously with freshly ground black pepper. Stir in a good pinch of nutmeg and a small pinch of chilli powder.

Heat the oven to 200°C/400°F/Gas 6. Grease a 2.5 l/4½ pint loaf tin. Line the bottom with sole fillets, spread in a layer of stuffing, then a layer of salmon. Carry on alternating layers, ending with a layer of stuffing. Knock the tin a couple of times on the work surface to ensure it is well-packed.

Line a large baking tin with a folded newspaper. Put the loaf tin in the centre of the baking tin. Pour in boiling water to come halfway up the sides of the loaf tin and cook the terrine in this *bain-marie* for approximately 1 hour, until the top feels firm. Leave the terrine to get cold, then cover and weigh down. Refrigerate for at least 3 hours and up to 48 hours.

Prepare the sauce. Wash and trim the watercress and herbs. Drain well and process quickly. Just before serving, whisk the *crème fraîche* in a bowl, then gradually stir in the herb mixture, whisking it well in. Squeeze in the lemon juice. Season the sauce with a little black pepper and spoon it into a sauceboat. Now unmould the terrine into the centre of a large serving dish. Surround with the prawns and sprigs of parsley or watercress. Serve with the sauce.

PAINS DE POISSON
Fish Loaves

In President de Gaulle's brave new France circa 1960, modern women like my mother, ex-career girls now full-time wives and mothers, were busy swopping colourful recipes that were at the time a little daring – in their relaxed use of canned food, spices and foreign, exotic ingredients. *Plats uniques* became the in-thing for dinner parties, with *paella* playing a starring role. *Elle* magazine's legendary cooking *Comtesse*, Mapie de Toulouse-Lautrec led the trend. So thrilled was I to learn that Mapie was a *diminutif* of Marie-Pierre that I tried to get everyone to call me Mapie too.

The following fish loaves are typical of the period. There was a sharp difference between family food – thrifty, filling but experimental – and dishes for entertaining – elaborately garnished and evidently more expensive. The basic fish loaf recipe was purely for family use. Note that it lists ketchup amongst its ingredients, the first recorded use of the stuff in my home-grown cookery cards. Fish loaf and assorted jokes about yet another biblical miracle on the shores of the Loire became a family institution.

The second recipe was *pour les invités* – for guests. I still prefer it to the basic dish, but, then, wouldn't I just?

PAIN DE POISSON DE TOUS LES JOURS
Family Fish Loaf

Serves 6

450 g/1 lb white fish, skinned and boned

1 bay leaf

1 bouquet garni

sea salt

freshly ground black pepper

1 × 60 g/2 oz can tomato purée

2 tablespoons tomato ketchup

5 eggs

paprika

cayenne pepper

oil for greasing

60 g/2 oz/4 tablespoons butter

Put the fish with the bay leaf and bouquet garni in a sauté pan. Cover with cold water, season with salt and freshly ground black pepper, bring to the boil, then simmer until the flesh is tender enough to flake easily. Drain well, remove any bones and put through a *mouli* or food processor. Stir in the tomato purée and ketchup.

Beat the eggs as for an omelette. Stir them into the fish mixture until well blended. Season with a good pinch each of paprika and cayenne.

Heat the oven to 180°C/350°F/Gas 4. Grease a large loaf tin, 2.5 1/4½ pints/12½ cups. Pour the mixture into the tin. Line a large baking tin with a folded newspaper. Put the loaf tin in the centre of the baking tin. Pour boiling water to come halfway up the sides of the loaf tin and cook the fish loaf in this *bain-marie* for 40 minutes, or until firm.

Unmould the fish loaf on to a dish. Melt the butter in a small saucepan and pour over the fish loaf just before serving.

PAIN DE POISSON POUR INVITÉS
Posh Fish Loaf

2 large white Spanish onions

3 tablespoons olive oil, plus extra for greasing

1 kg/2¼ lb tomatoes

1 clove of garlic

several sprigs of thyme, marjoram and parsley

dried oregano

1.8 kg/4 lbs cod or hake, skinned and boned

Serves 8

3 thin slices of cooked ham

200 g/7 oz green olives, stoned

5–6 eggs

sea salt

freshly ground black pepper

paprika

cayenne pepper

2 sweet red peppers

To serve

120 g/4 oz/8 tablespoons butter

½ lemon

or

35 ml/12 fl oz/1½ cups hollandaise (page 12)

Prepare a tomato sauce. Chop the onions. Heat 1 tablespoon olive oil in a frying-pan and sauté the onions over a low heat, stirring frequently. Blanch, skin, halve and seed the tomatoes. Chop roughly with the garlic and add to the onions. Add the herbs and cook gently for 20–30 minutes. Remove the sprigs of herbs from the pan, then process the sauce in a food processor or put through a *mouli*.

Meanwhile, cook the fish. Heat 1 tablespoon olive oil in a sauté pan. Cut the fish into large pieces and add these to the pan. Sauté over a gentle heat until cooked. Drain the pieces on absorbent paper, removing any visible bones, then put in a large bowl and shred finely with a fork. Stir the tomato sauce into the shredded fish, and beat until well mixed.

Finely chop the ham and green olives, then add them to the fish and tomato mixture, stirring until combined. Beat the eggs as for an omelette. Season lightly with salt and freshly ground black pepper, then beat into the mixture. Season to taste with paprika and cayenne, salt and black pepper.

Grease a large loaf tin with the rest of the oil. Pour the mixture into the tin and bake as in the previous recipe for 30–40 minutes, until cooked. The fish loaf will stay warm for up to 15 minutes in the tin outside the oven.

Meanwhile, prepare the peppers. Cut them in half lengthways, remove the seeds, and white cores, then char them under a hot grill until the skins blister. Leave until they are cool enough to handle, then peel off the skins. Now slice them into even-sized narrow strips.

Just before serving, unmould the loaf into a dish. Arrange the strips of red pepper on top of the loaf and around it. Melt the butter in a small saucepan, squeeze in the lemon juice and spoon over the fish loaf and peppers: alternatively, coat with hollandaise. This dish can also be served cold with a light mayonnaise.

LA POULE AU POT FARCIE/**Stuffed Boiled Chicken**

POULET AU VINAIGRE/**Chicken with a Vinegar Sauce**

COQ AU VIN/**Chicken Cooked in Red Wine**

POULARDE À LA TOURANGELLE
Chicken Cooked in a Wine and Cream Sauce

POULET CHASSEUR/**Huntsman's Chicken**

CHAUDFROID DE POULET/**Chicken** Chaudfroid

PERDREAUX EN CASSEROLE/**Pot-roasted Partridges**

MAGRETS DE CANARD À L'ORANGE
Duck Breasts with Orange

CANARD AUX PÊCHES/**Roast Duck with Peaches**

CANARD AUX OLIVES/**Duck with Olives**

CANARD AUX NAVETS/**Braised Duck with Turnips**

FAISAN RÔTI FARCI/**Stuffed Roast Pheasant**

TERRINE DE FAISAN/**Pheasant Terrine**

LAPIN EN DAUBE/**Pot-roasted Rabbit**

LAPIN À LA MOUTARDE/**Rabbit with Mustard**

LAPIN À LA BIÈRE ET AUX PRUNEAUX
Rabbit with Ale and Prunes

CIVET DE LIÈVRE/**Jugged Hare**

BLANQUETTE DE VEAU
Veal in a Cream and Mushroom Sauce

VEAU AUX GIROLLES/**Veal with Wild Mushrooms**

CÔTES DE PORC AU CIDRE ET À L'OIGNON
Pan-fried Pork Chops with Onion and Vinegar

PORC À LA BOULANGÈRE/**Roast Pork with Potatoes**

CASSOULET MAISON/**Pork and Haricot Beans Casserole**

GIGOT/**Leg of Lamb**

AGNEAU EN PAPILLOTE/**Marinated Lamb Parcels**

NAVARIN D'AGNEAU/**Lamb Stew with Turnips**

TAGINE DE MOUTON YONNÉE
Lamb Pot-roast with Onions and Raisins

ROGNONS AU VIN ROUGE/**Kidneys in Red Wine**

BŒUF BOURGUIGNON/**Beef Cooked in Red Burgundy**

BŒUF EN DAUBE/**Slow-cooked Beef Casserole**

POT AU FEU/**Boiled Beef with Vegetables**

BŒUF MODE/**Braised Beef**

STEAKS AU POIVRE ET AUX ANCHOIS
Steaks with Pepper and Anchovy

HACHIS PARMENTIER/**French Cottage Pie**

Volailles et Viandes
Poultry, Game and Meat

The times may be a-changing, but the meat course still remains the centre-piece of the French meal – the dish you just don't do without, even when time and appetite are limited.

The following selection is a very personal one. I give you recipes that have been with me for much of my life and which I am always happy to cook. Pot-roasts and stews tend to steal the show, perhaps because, when I close my eyes and think of a kitchen, sooner or later a large black cast iron *cocotte* materialises. It never goes away. The *cocotte* is the crucible of the French kitchen, well-tempered and endlessly accommodating. I could go on happily about the miracles it performs, but a great deal has already been written, and very well too, on the romance of the *cocotte*, so I won't dwell on it. Do go and buy one, though, or get to know yours, if you have one already. You will not regret it.

Meat is an expensive commodity, even more so if it turns out a culinary disappointment. For this reason I only buy pre-packed supermarket meat and poultry if I have to. There is no pleasure in it. I feel very strongly that the buying of meat should be a personal transaction. As a child or teenager, when I was dispatched on a shopping expedition, I was generally trusted to return with more or less the right groceries, vegetables and fruit. Cheeses I was instructed to buy from one known shop, with the help of one particular assistant. But when it came to meat, my role was that of humble courier. The deal had always been discussed on the phone first, by my grandmother or my mother. The day's requirements had been carefully explained and the previous purchase commented on.

Whenever I go to a butcher's in France, I always feel that the queueing is endless. The butchers and their customers seem to chat forever. It takes a while to re-adjust to the fact that nobody wants to rush the occasion. Buying meat is an important purchase that takes up a lot of the family's food budget. It needs to be given due consideration. Fortunately, things being what they are, queueing at the butcher's is also a nice social occasion, time for a little moan and a good gossip . . .

La Poule au Pot Farcie
Stuffed Boiled Chicken

A GREAT ONE-POT dish. All it takes is a little patience as the chicken must be allowed to simmer extremely slowly indeed.

1 large chicken, with its giblets for the stuffing

¼ Savoy or white cabbage

sea salt

450 g/1 lb carrots

400 g/14 oz turnips

10 small–medium leeks

1 head of celery

several sprigs of parsley and thyme

2 bay leaves

freshly ground black pepper

Serves 6

FOR THE STUFFING

225 g/8 oz thick-cut smoked bacon

200 g/7 oz cooked ham

200 g/7 oz/2½ cups breadcrumbs made from day-old bread

2 cloves of garlic

several sprigs of parsley

2 eggs

sea salt

freshly ground black pepper

TO SERVE

gherkins

mustard

coarse sea salt

PREPARE THE STUFFING. COMBINE together the liver, heart and gizzard, bacon and ham with the breadcrumbs, garlic and parsley in a food processor. Add the eggs to the bowl and process briefly. Season lightly with salt and more generously with freshly ground black pepper. Spoon the stuffing into the cavity. Sew up the cavity with a trussing needle and fine string, then truss the chicken with string.

Put the chicken in a very large heavy-based saucepan or flameproof casserole. Cover with cold water and very gently bring to the boil over a low heat, skimming the surface as and when necessary. Prepare the vegetables while the bird is coming to the boil. Blanch the cabbage for a few minutes in lightly salted boiling water. Peel the carrots and turnips.

Carefully wash and trim the leeks and celery and tie them together in bundles.

As soon as the water starts to boil, add the vegetables to the pot. Season with salt. Bring back to a low boil, and simmer for 2–2½ hours, skimming whenever necessary.

Just before serving, remove the chicken from the pot. Discard the strings and remove the stuffing from the bird. Cut the stuffing into pieces. Serve the chicken in a large dish surrounded by the vegetables and stuffing. Strain the cooking liquid through a sieve, lined with a muslin or fine cloth. Check the seasoning and use a little strained liquid to moisten the bird and vegetables. Transfer the rest to a sauceboat. Serve with gherkins, mustard and coarse sea salt.

POULET AU VINAIGRE
Chicken with a Vinegar Sauce

ALONG WITH *FLIC*, *poulet* is one of the many words the French use to refer to a member of their police force. Film-maker Claude Chabrol called one of his enjoyable piquant thrillers *Poulet au Vinaigre* – which somebody cleverly rendered into English as *Cop au Vin*, very passable menu French, if you ask me. I have wondered ever since if Monsieur Chabrol, a gourmet of great repute, had any strong views on the dish . . . This is not his recipe.

Serves 4–6

1 large chicken
2 tablespoons olive oil
1 tablespoon butter
2 cloves of garlic
sea salt
freshly ground black pepper
1 tablespoon Dijon mustard
1 tablespoon tomato purée
3 tablespoons dry white wine
4 tablespoons good quality
white wine vinegar
3 tablespoons double cream

JOINT THE CHICKEN. HEAT THE OIL and butter in a large sauté pan. Cut the cloves of garlic in half. Put the jointed chicken in the pan with the garlic and sauté for several minutes, turning the pieces over to colour lightly and evenly. Season sparsely with salt and freshly ground black pepper, cover and cook gently for 20–30 minutes, until the chicken pieces are cooked through. Keep the heat low and shake the pan several times during the cooking.

Meanwhile, mix together in a bowl the mustard, tomato purée and white wine. When the chicken is cooked, sprinkle the vinegar into the pan; stir for a few minutes until the liquid has reduced. Cover and leave over a low heat.

Remove the chicken from the pan and keep warm. Add the mustard mixture to the pan, turn up the heat a little, and stir for a couple of minutes. Spoon in the cream, and heat through gently, stirring occasionally. Pour the sauce over the chicken and serve immediately.

COQ AU VIN
Chicken Cooked in Red Wine

I LOVE COOKING casseroles on the top of the stove, lifting the lid, nosing the mixture and giving it an encouraging stir or two, as it melts and blends into a rich comforting dish. *Coq au vin* is one of my favourites. I find it so enjoyable to re-discover that I never quite cook it exactly the same way. The addition of chocolate to the ingredients is a recent one, inspired by reading Raymonde Charlon, formerly of *La Godille* in Brittany. Madame Charlon's little trick does add a distinct *je ne sais quoi* to the old classic.

	Serves 6	
1 large chicken		225 g/8 oz button mushrooms
2 tablespoons oil		30 g/1 oz bitter chocolate
30 g/1 oz/2 tablespoons butter, plus extra to finish the sauce	90 ml/3 fl oz/⅓ cup brandy	a few sprigs each of parsley and thyme
120 g/4 oz thick-cut smoked bacon	1 tablespoon flour	2 bay leaves
	600 ml/1 pint/2½ cups Burgundy red wine	sea salt
1 large white Spanish onion		freshly ground black pepper
2 shallots	2 cloves of garlic	

JOINT THE CHICKEN. HEAT THE OIL AND butter in a large flameproof casserole or heavy-based saucepan. Chop the bacon, onion and shallots and sauté in the hot oil until lightly coloured. Push to the sides and add the chicken pieces. Sauté the chicken until golden, turning the pieces over to colour evenly.

As soon as the chicken is a nice golden colour, pour in the brandy and carefully set alight. Once the flames have died down, sprinkle in the flour and stir well with a wooden spoon. Pour in the wine. Finely chop the garlic, slice the mushrooms and roughly grate the chocolate. Add them all to the chicken with the sprigs of herbs and the bay leaves. Stir well.

Turn up the heat and bring to a fast simmer, then cover and reduce the heat to moderately low. Cook for a good 30 minutes or until the chicken pieces are cooked, shaking the pan occasionally. Season to taste with salt and freshly ground black pepper. This dish tastes even better reheated and will benefit from being made in the morning – or even one day – ahead. Reheat very gently, adding a little water if necessary – but not too much.

Serve the chicken in the casserole. Remove the chicken pieces with tongs and put them on a plate. Discard the sprigs of herbs and bay leaves.

Turn up the heat and reduce the sauce a little if it looks too thin, scraping the bottom of the casserole with a wooden spoon or spatula. Stir in a good knob of butter, then return the chicken to the casserole and serve at once.

POULARDE À LA TOURANGELLE
Chicken Cooked in a Wine and Cream Sauce

A DELICATE *FRICASSÉE* from the Loire, where it is often made with guinea fowl and Vouvray rather than just chicken and white wine . . . For me, this dish typifies the cooking of the area, fragrant, unpretentious and making the most of the excellent local produce.

1 chicken or guinea fowl, without giblets	Serves 4	sea salt
1 tablespoon oil		freshly ground black pepper
45 g/1½ oz/3 tablespoons butter		120 ml/4 fl oz/½ cup Vouvray or medium-dry white wine
1 onion	150 g/5 oz button mushrooms	100 ml/3½ fl oz/generous ⅓ cup single cream
2 rashers of thick-cut bacon	several sprigs each of thyme, parsley and chives	1 lemon
1 clove of garlic		2 small egg yolks

JOINT THE BIRD AND SOAK THE PIECES FOR a couple of hours in water at room temperature. Drain well and pat dry firmly with a clean cloth or absorbent paper.

In a sauté pan, heat the oil and butter. Chop up the onion and bacon. Sauté in the pan for a few minutes over a gentle heat, then push to the sides and add the chicken pieces. Sauté until they are lightly coloured all over.

Meanwhile, crush the garlic and slice the mushrooms. Add to the pan with the fresh herbs. Season lightly with salt and freshly ground black pepper. Moisten with the white wine, then partly cover and cook over a low heat until the chicken is cooked and the liquid well reduced – about 20–30 minutes.

Pour the cream into the pan and stir until heated through, then remove the chicken from the pan with tongs or a slotted spoon and keep warm on a serving dish. Squeeze the lemon and mix the juice with the egg yolks. Away from the heat, stir this mixture into the pan. Check the seasoning and spoon the sauce over the chicken. Serve immediately.

POULET CHASSEUR
Huntsman's Chicken

Wʜᴇɴ ɪ ꜰɪʀꜱᴛ ate *poulet chasseur*, I was also at the time endlessly listening to the first record I ever owned, *Peter and the Wolf*, narrated by Gérard Philipe (taking time off from *Fanfan La Tulipe*). So the dish stayed linked in my mind with the sound of horns and the picture of three very Russian huntsmen stalking through a forest . . . By the time I came across *pollo cacciatore* years later and opened my pocket Italian dictionary, I was ready to enjoy the fact that huntsmen and country dishes, like fairy tales, have much in common the world over.

4 chicken leg portions	Serves 4	sea salt
1 tablespoon oil		freshly ground black pepper
30 g/1 oz/2 tablespoons butter, plus extra to finish		2 tomatoes
3 shallots	3 tablespoons brandy	120 g/4 oz brown cap mushrooms
1 clove of garlic	100 ml/3½ fl oz/generous ⅓ cup dry white wine	several sprigs of chervil and tarragon
1 level tablespoon flour	chicken stock or water	

Hᴇᴀᴛ ᴛʜᴇ ᴏɪʟ ᴀɴᴅ ʙᴜᴛᴛᴇʀ. Fɪɴᴇʟʏ chop the shallots and garlic. Sauté the chicken pieces in the hot fat with the shallots and garlic, turning the pieces over to colour evenly.

Sprinkle the chicken pieces with the flour. Add the brandy, then the white wine and enough chicken stock or water to just cover the chicken. Stir well. Season with salt and freshly ground black pepper, cover and simmer over a moderate heat for 20–30 minutes. Shake the pan occasionally during cooking.

Meanwhile, blanch, skin, seed and roughly chop the tomatoes, then slice the mushrooms. Stir the tomatoes and mushrooms into the pan. Cover and simmer for 10 minutes, or until the chicken is cooked through. Remove the chicken from the pan and arrange on a serving dish. Keep warm while you finish off the sauce.

Turn up the heat to reduce the sauce. Snip the chervil and tarragon into the pan, stir well for a minute or two, then swirl in a good knob of butter. Check the seasoning and pour the sauce over the chicken pieces. Serve immediately.

CHAUDFROID DE POULET
Chicken Chaudfroid

A GOOD PARTY dish, particularly popular, if my memory serves me right, with elderly members of the family.

	Serves 8–10	
2 large chickens		freshly ground black pepper
2 carrots		60 g/2 oz/4 tablespoons butter
2 turnips		4 tablespoons flour
2 leeks		300 ml/½ pint/1¼ cups *crème fraîche* or double cream
1 onion	3 cloves	
several sprigs of parsley and tarragon, plus extra tarragon to finish the dish	250 ml/8 fl oz/1 cup white wine	4 egg yolks
	sea salt	1–2 lemons

THE DAY BEFORE YOU INTEND TO SERVE THE dish, place the chickens side by side in a very large heavy-based saucepan. Peel, wash and coarsely chop the carrots, turnips, leeks and onion and add to the pan with the parsley, tarragon and cloves. Pour in the wine, and enough cold water to cover the chickens and vegetables.

Bring gently to a boil, skimming off any scum that may come up to the surface. Season lightly with salt and freshly ground black pepper. Simmer for 45–60 minutes over a very moderate heat, until the chickens are cooked through. Leave them in the liquid until cool enough to handle, then lift the chickens out of the pot, drain well and remove the skins. Leave the birds to get cold before jointing them as neatly as possible. Meanwhile carefully strain the stock into a saucepan through a sieve lined with a piece of muslin or fine cloth, and reserve for the sauce.

To make the sauce, bring the reserved stock to a simmer. Take off the heat. Melt the butter in another saucepan. Add the flour and cook for a couple of minutes, stirring vigorously to make a light roux. Pour in the hot chicken stock gradually, then bring to the boil, still stirring vigorously. Reduce the heat and simmer for about 10 minutes, stirring occasionally.

Remove the pan from the heat and allow to cool a little. Stir the cream into the sauce. Beat the egg yolks, and squeeze the lemon or lemons. Beat a couple of spoonfuls of the hot sauce into the egg yolks, then stir the mixture into the sauce, and continue stirring for a while. Season to taste with lemon juice, salt and freshly ground black pepper.

Pat the chicken pieces dry with absorbent paper and arrange on a large serving dish. Using a ladle, coat them evenly with the sauce. Chill the dish overnight and serve sprinkled with tarragon leaves.

PERDREAUX EN CASSEROLE
Pot-roasted Partridges

A RECIPE FROM my mother. The sauce is best finished off with slightly bitter orange juice. So, if Sevilles aren't in season, taste it and, if it seems on the sweet side, add a dash of lemon or lime juice.

	Serves 4	
2 oven-ready partridges		sea salt
60 g/2 oz/4 tablespoons butter		freshly ground black pepper
a few sprigs of parsley and thyme		cayenne pepper
1 bay leaf		120 g/4 oz cured raw ham, thinly cut
1 heaped tablespoon flour		2 Seville oranges, or 1 large juicy orange
250 ml/8 fl oz/1 cup white wine		

ORANGES DE BLANCHARD

HEAT THE BUTTER IN A FLAMEPROOF casserole. Over a moderate heat, sauté the partridges until brown on all sides. Remove them from the pan with a slotted spoon, allowing the juices to drip back into the pan. Reserve the partridges. Snip the parsley, thyme and bay leaf.

Sprinkle the flour into the pan, stir until slightly coloured, then pour in the white wine and add the herbs. Season with a very little salt and freshly ground black pepper and a small pinch of cayenne. Cook, stirring vigorously, until the liquid begins to bubble. Reduce the heat a little and simmer for a good 5 minutes, stirring occasionally. Return the partridges to the pan, cover and simmer very gently over a low heat for about 20 minutes.

Meanwhile, chop the ham into small pieces. Squeeze the juice from the orange or oranges into a bowl.

Transfer the partridges on to a hot serving dish. Add the ham and orange juice to the pan, stir until heated through, scraping up the sediments from the bottom of the pan, then pour the sauce over the partridges. Serve immediately.

MAGRETS DE CANARD À L'ORANGE
Duck Breasts with Orange

*C*ANARD À L'ORANGE had become such a tired cliché by the Seventies that we all heaved a sigh of relief when it was knocked off the menu by very rare *magrets* dramatically arranged on a bed of red fruit sauce. Now that these too have palled, may I suggest these duck breasts with orange. They are quick to cook, quicker still if, unlike me, you prefer them pink. The little orange, lemon and Cointreau sauce, is adapted from my mother's much sweeter original recipe.

Serves 4

2 large, boned duck breasts, each
weighing about 350 g/12 oz

sea salt

freshly ground black pepper

2 oranges

1 lemon

1 scant teaspoon cornflour

4 tablespoons Cointreau

With a small and very sharp knife, score the skin side of the duck breasts – deeply enough to cut into the flesh – several times in long parallel lines. Season with salt and freshly ground black pepper. Heat a heavy-based frying-pan until hot. Put the breasts in the pan skin-side down (there is enough fat in the skin to need no extra). Cook for a good 10 minutes over a moderate heat.

Meanwhile, peel one of the oranges and the lemon. Chop the zests very finely and blanch for a couple of minutes in a little boiling water, then drain well. Squeeze the oranges and lemon.

After about 10 minutes, turn over the duck breasts. Lower and cook them for 4–6 minutes on the flesh side – the timing will depend on how well-cooked you like your duck. Remove the breasts from the pan and set aside to relax, keeping them hot on a heated serving dish under a heated plate.

Pour some of the fat out of the pan, stir in the cornflour, then add the orange and lemon juices, and the drained, finely chopped peel. Stir for a couple of minutes over a moderate heat, until simmering, then add the Cointreau and season with a little salt and more generously with freshly ground black pepper. Spoon or pour the sauce over the duck breasts and serve immediately.

CANARD AUX PÊCHES
Roast Duck with Peaches

My father's recipe, and very good and mellow it is too. Peaches canned in juice are worth looking out for, otherwise rinse the peaches quickly under the tap (after draining off the syrup) to get rid of the excess sweetness.

1.8–2.3 kg/4–5 lb oven-ready duck	Serves 4	1 large can white peaches, drained and halved
sea salt		3 tablespoons double cream
freshly ground black pepper		3 tablespoons brandy

Heat the oven to 180°C/350°F/GAS 4. Rinse the duck well inside and out, and pat dry with absorbent paper. Score the skin with the point of a sharp knife or skewer. Season the bird well inside and out with salt and freshly ground black pepper.

Stuff the cavity through the tail end with the cream and some of the peaches, reserving the rest. Put the duck on a rack in a roasting tin, and roast in the oven for 1½ hours. After half an hour, prick the skin, baste the duck with the cooking juices and add the rest of the peaches to the roasting tin. Baste the duck again occasionally.

When the duck is cooked, lift the rack off the roasting tin. Arrange the peaches from the roasting tin on a serving dish. Discard much of the fat. Spoon the stuffing out of the cavity into the roasting tin. Add the duck and the peaches used in the stuffing to the serving dish. Place the tin over a moderate heat and pour in the brandy. Stir the mixture for 2 minutes, scraping the bottom of the tin. Strain the sauce into a sauceboat, season lightly and serve.

CANARD AUX OLIVES
Duck with Olives

A pleasant way of braising duck. I sometimes use the same method for chicken and serve it with rice and mushrooms.

1.8–2.3 kg/4–5 lb oven-ready duck	Serves 4	a few sprigs of thyme
sea salt		1 bay leaf
freshly ground black pepper	30 g/1 oz/2 tablespoons butter	1 large white Spanish onion
1 tablespoon oil	300 ml/½ pint/1¼ cups dry white wine	2 large tomatoes
		225 g/8 oz stoned green olives

Rinse the duck well, inside and out, and pat dry with absorbent paper. Season inside and out with salt and freshly ground black pepper. In a large flameproof casserole heat the oil and butter. Sauté the duck in the hot fat until the skin is crisp and golden on all sides.

Spoon a couple of tablespoons of hot fat into a frying-pan and discard the rest. Add the wine and herbs to the duck, cover and reduce the heat. Cook gently for 30 minutes, basting the duck once or twice. Meanwhile, chop the onion and tomatoes and sauté in the reserved duck fat over a low heat until softened, stirring occasionally. Stir the onion and tomato mixture into the casserole, then cover and simmer for a further 30 minutes.

Stir in the olives, and a little water if the mixture looks too dry. Cover and simmer for another half hour. Serve very hot.

CANARD AUX NAVETS
Braised Duck with Turnips

I DON'T KNOW where the marriage of duck and turnips was made, but it is certainly a happy one. Having tried a number of approaches to the dish, I now feel that dividing the turnips between the pot and the frying-pan produces the best results, even if it is slightly more fiddly. If you don't like turnips, replace them with baby onions.

1.8–2.3 kg/4–5 lb oven-ready duck	Serves 4–5	30 g/1 oz/2 tablespoons butter, plus extra to finish the sauce
sea salt		250 ml/8 fl oz/1 cup chicken or vegetable stock
freshly ground black pepper		2–3 teaspoons sugar
1 kg/2¼ lbs baby turnips		60 ml/4 tablespoons/¼ cup white wine
1 tablespoon oil		

RINSE THE DUCK WELL INSIDE AND OUT, and pat dry with absorbent paper. Season well inside and out with salt and freshly ground black pepper. Peel the turnips and cut them neatly into halves or quarters, depending on size. Reserve 8–10 pieces and cook the rest in lightly salted boiling water for 5–10 minutes.

Meanwhile, in a large flameproof casserole or heavy-based saucepan, heat the oil and butter. Sauté the duck in the hot fat until lightly golden on all sides. Pour out the fat into a frying-pan to use for browning the turnips. Add the stock and the reserved turnips to the pan with the duck. Cover tightly and cook over a low heat for about 1½ hours.

Drain the first batch of turnips and set aside. When the duck is nearly cooked, heat the fat in the frying-pan and add the turnips. Sprinkle them with the sugar and sauté gently for 15–20 minutes over a low heat, shaking the pan occasionally and turning the turnips over.

Remove the duck from its pan and arrange it and the sautéed turnips on a serving dish. Keep this dish warm. Turn up the heat, add the white wine to the duck stock and let the cooking liquid reduce a little, stirring well and mashing the turnips roughly with the back of a wooden spoon. Season with salt and freshly ground black pepper. Strain some of the sauce over the duck and the rest into a bowl or sauceboat (discarding the remaining mashed turnips). Stir a little butter into the sauceboat to finish and serve hot with the duck and sautéed turnips.

Faisan Rôti Farci
Stuffed Roast Pheasant

Like millions of other Frenchmen, my father used to go shooting regularly on a Sunday, so pheasant often featured on our menu during the autumn and winter months. Far too often it seemed, to his daughters. We much preferred chicken and said so loudly every time its elegant relative appeared on the table. In the end my mother gave up setting pearls in front of her piglets and served pheasant to her dinner party guests instead.

1 plump pheasant, dressed, gizzards reserved

4 thin rashers of streaky green bacon

1 extremely small jar or tin of truffle parings

3 tablespoons of brandy

Serves 2–4

1 tablespoon of breadcrumbs made with day-old bread

75g/2½ oz/5 tablespoons butter

sea salt

freshly ground black pepper

4 thick pieces of bread

Heat the oven to 220°C/425°F/GAS 7. Prepare the stuffing. Rinse the gizzards, and process them quickly with 1 rasher of bacon, the truffle parings and their juice, 1 tablespoon of brandy, the breadcrumbs and a good knob of butter in a food processor. Season with a little salt and freshly ground black pepper. Rinse the cavity of the pheasant and pat it dry with absorbent paper. Spoon the stuffing into the cavity, then sew it up, using a trussing needle and fine string.

Stretch the remaining bacon rashers with the help of a rolling pin or palette knife. Wrap the bird well in the rashers and tie with string.

Toast the bread very lightly. Melt the rest of the butter in a small saucepan. Lay the toasted bread pieces on the bottom of a roasting tin. Stand a rack in the tin and place the pheasant on the rack. Trickle a little melted butter over the pheasant. Return the saucepan to a warm place.

Roast the pheasant in the oven for about 50 minutes, occasionally dribbling a little more melted butter over it. If the bread looks as if about to burn, remove it from the tin and reserve in a warm place. Remove the bacon larding and discard with the strings, or reserve the bacon for a salad. Add the rest of the brandy to the melted butter. Return the bread to the tin if necessary.

Dribble the butter and brandy mixture over the pheasant, season lightly with salt and freshly ground black pepper and return to the oven for another 5–10 minutes, until golden brown.

To serve, cut off and discard the string from the cavity. Carefully extract the stuffing from the pheasant and divide it between the pieces of buttery toast. Arrange the toast and stuffing with the pheasant, on a serving dish.

Serve hot.

Terrine de Faisan
Pheasant Terrine

La terrine maison. We tend to help ourselves from the dish, not terribly elegantly, and serve bread, butter and gherkins with it.

For special occasions, however, this terrine looks most presentable, unmoulded on to a gleaming platter, cut into thin overlapping slices and surrounded by a small border of chopped aspic and tiny bouquets of parsley.

Serves 8

1 plump pheasant	100 ml/3½ fl oz/generous ⅓ cup brandy or marc	1 bay leaf
500 g/1 lb 2 oz lean spare rib of pork	2 large eggs	6 black peppercorns
a few sprigs of thyme	6 thin rashers of smoked streaky bacon	300 ml/½ pint/1¼ cups dry white wine
3 sage leaves		1 envelope (30 g/1 oz/1 heaped tablespoon) good commercial savoury aspic powder
1 bay leaf	For the aspic	
3 cloves of garlic	2 carrots	2 teaspoons brandy
sea salt	several sprigs of thyme, parsley and chervil	2 tablespoons Madeira
freshly ground black pepper		

Heat the oven to 170°C/325°F/gas 3. Joint and bone the pheasant. Reserve the breast fillets, and also set aside the bones. Bone and trim the pork, again reserving the bones.

Finely mince, or quickly whizz together, the pheasant meat (including the liver), the pork, thyme, sage and bay leaves and the garlic in a food processor. Season the minced meat mixture with a little salt and more generously with freshly ground black pepper. Stir in the brandy and the eggs and work the mixture well, preferably with your hands.

Stretch the bacon rashers with the help of a rolling pin or palette knife. Line a terrine dish (or a loaf tin) with a couple of bacon rashers, then spread in an even layer of meat and egg mixture. Cut the breast fillets into neat long strips, and place 2–3 strips over the meat/egg layer. Cover with another layer of meat mixture then place another layer of breast fillets on top. Spread in another layer of meat mixture, then cover with bacon rashers. Cover the dish tightly.

Line a large roasting-tin with a thick layer of newspapers. Place the dish in the middle of the tin. Pour in boiling water to come halfway up the sides of the dish. Carefully put the tin in the oven and bake for a good 3 hours, pouring in more boiling water as and when necessary to keep the halfway level.

While the terrine is in the oven, prepare the aspic. Peel the carrots. Put the reserved bones in a large saucepan with the peeled carrots, the sprigs of herbs, the bay leaf and the peppercorns. Cover with the white wine and 850 ml/1½ pints/3¾ cups cold water. Slowly bring to the boil, skimming off any greasy scum that comes up to the surface. Partly cover and simmer gently for a couple of hours, skimming off occasionally. Turn up the heat towards the end – you should end up with 600 ml/1 pint/2½ cups stock. Strain through a sieve lined with a muslin, or through a *chinois*, into a bowl. Stand the bowl in cold water to cool.

Leave the terrine to relax in the oven for a quarter of an hour after you turn off the heat. Remove from the oven, take off the cover and leave for a few minutes. Meanwhile, transfer the stock to a saucepan, stir in the aspic powder and bring to the boil, whisking constantly. Remove from the heat and stir in the brandy and Madeira.

Remove the rashers of bacon from the top of the terrine. Pierce it deeply in several places with a skewer. Pour over the warm aspic liquid. Leave to cool and refrigerate overnight.

LAPIN EN DAUBE
Pot-roasted Rabbit

A USEFUL DISH that slowly cooks all by itself. I have been vaguer than usual about the timing, since it will depend entirely on the age and provenance of your rabbit. If you prefer, follow exactly the same method but use hare, kid or chicken.

Serves 4

1 rabbit, jointed, or 4–6 rabbit pieces

6 thick-cut rashers of smoked streaky bacon

1 large white Spanish onion

1 carrot

several sprigs each of parsley, thyme and rosemary

2 bay leaves

3 juniper berries

2 cloves of garlic

sea salt

freshly ground black pepper

150 ml/¼ pint/⅔ cup dry white wine

HEAT THE OVEN TO 150°C/300°F/GAS 2. Flatten and stretch the rashers of bacon with the help of a rolling pin – I wrap my old wooden one in cling film first in the interests of hygiene. Line the bottom of a medium-sized casserole with 3 rashers and reserve the rest.

Slice the onion and carrot and arrange the slices on the bacon. Snip half the herbs over the vegetables, add the rabbit pieces, then the bay leaves and juniper berries. Crush the garlic and put on top of the rabbit pieces. Snip in the rest of the herbs. Season with a little salt and more generously with freshly ground black pepper. Moisten with the wine. Cover with the rest of the bacon rashers.

Cover the dish and cook in the oven for 2–3 hours, until the rabbit is very tender. Serve piping hot.

LAPIN À LA MOUTARDE
Rabbit with Mustard

I STILL LOVE mustard and am known to surreptitiously use it with roast chicken or lamb, but over the years, my *lapin à la moutarde* has become gradually milder. The recipe below is the state of the art at the moment. In the old days, I stirred in an extra couple of tablespoons of milder mustard before adding the liquid to the browned and floured rabbit. Try it both ways and also experiment with different mustards until you get the results you like best.

1 rabbit, jointed, or 4–6 rabbit pieces	**Serves 4**	200 ml/7 fl oz/generous ¾ cup chicken stock or white wine, plus extra liquid if needed
1 tablespoon oil		3 tablespoons brandy
45 g/1½ oz/3 tablespoons butter, plus extra to finish	1 clove of garlic	3 tablespoons strong Dijon mustard, or your favourite mustard
sea salt	2 shallots	
freshly ground black pepper	a few sprigs each of thyme and rosemary	120 ml/4 fl oz/½ cup single cream
1 tablespoon flour		a few sprigs of parsley, to finish

HEAT THE OIL AND BUTTER IN A FLAME-proof casserole or sauté pan. Add the rabbit pieces to the pan, season with salt and freshly ground black pepper and sprinkle in the flour. Sauté for a few minutes, turning the pieces over regularly. Crush the garlic and finely chop the shallots. Add to the pan. Snip in the thyme and rosemary.

Moisten with the chicken stock or white wine, stir, and cook, covered, over a low heat for about 45 minutes – the exact timing will depend on the rabbit you are using. Shake the pan occasionally and reduce the heat if necessary – rabbit pieces tend to shred and stick all to

easily to the bottom of pans. Moisten with a little extra liquid if needed. Heat the brandy and pour it over the rabbit. Set alight, then remove the rabbit pieces from the pan and keep them warm on a plate or serving dish while you finish the sauce.

Remove the sprigs of thyme and rosemary. Stir in the mustard and the cream. Heat for a couple of minutes, still stirring.

Snip in the parsley and swirl in a good-sized knob of butter, then pour the sauce over the rabbit. If you prefer to serve the rabbit from the pan, gently stir the pieces into the sauce instead.

Lapin à la Bière et aux Pruneaux
Rabbit with Ale and Prunes

Having once overheard grown-ups exchanging dire tales of myxomatosis, and not realizing that they were reminiscing and that the big epidemic was a thing of the past, I spent my childhood carefully avoiding rabbits, both in the hutch and on the plate. What a good thing I missed out on. This recipe converted me in the end. If you share my early phobia, don't give up on this rich, dark dish. For rabbit read pork, or stewing steak: the recipe is excellent for cheaper cuts of beef. Trim off as much visible fat as possible, and double the cooking time.

This dish tastes even better if allowed to mature for a day or two in the refrigerator. Add the mustard toast when you start reheating. Serve with rice – or with potatoes, particularly if you are using beef rather than rabbit.

1 rabbit, cut into 4–6 pieces (about 800 g/1¾ lbs)	**Serves 4**	2 tablespoons wine vinegar
flour for coating		sea salt
2 tablespoons oil	several sprigs of thyme	freshly ground black pepper
225 g/8 oz thick-cut smoked bacon	2 bay leaves	To serve
1 medium-sized onion	600 ml/1 pint/2½ cups brown ale	1 large slice *pain de campagne* or Granary bread toast
	175 g/6 oz moist stoned prunes	Dijon mustard

Coat the rabbit pieces lightly with flour. Heat the oil in a heavy-based flameproof casserole or large saucepan. Add the rabbit pieces and gently sauté until golden, turning them over to brown evenly.

Cut the bacon into small 2.5 cm/1 in pieces and chop the onion. Add bacon and onion to the sautéed rabbit pieces with the thyme and bay leaves. Sprinkle with a little extra flour, stir well, then pour in the ale. Partly cover the casserole and cook for about 40 minutes over a low heat. Add the prunes and wine vinegar, give a good stir and continue to cook for 20 minutes. Again, leave the lid only partly covering the casserole.

Taste and season the sauce. Generously spread Dijon mustard over both sides of the piece of toast and add to the casserole. Cover completely and cook for a further 10 minutes before serving.

Civet de Lièvre
Jugged Hare

To make a proper jugged hare, you need to collect the blood as you skin and gut the animal. This you use to make a liaison which enriches and finishes off this 'noble dish'. You also need 'your two best bottles of red wine'. The incomparable Edouard de Pomiane whose words I am humbly borrowing had only one regret – that he was not wealthy enough to 'make a civet with Chambertin' . . . Back in Touraine, we use Bourgueil, one bottle to cook with and one (or two) to drink with the dish.

If you aren't able to get hold of a whole hare, complete with blood, use a little *beurre manié* made by mashing together flour and butter (see page 12) to thicken the sauce. And if you can't find a hare, use rabbit instead. The marinade does wonders for even the toughest of bunnies. It won't be quite the real thing but it will still be a marvellous casserole.

This dish is traditionally served with croûtons.

	Serves 6	
1 hare		1 tablespoon oil
1 bottle of good red wine		45 g/1½ oz/3 tablespoons butter
60 ml/4 tablespoons/¼ cup brandy		1 tablespoon flour
2 cloves of garlic	3 bay leaves	sea salt
1 large white Spanish onion	6 black peppercorns	freshly ground black pepper
several sprigs each of thyme and parsley	4 thick-cut rashers of smoked streaky bacon	225 g/8 oz button mushrooms
		croûtons, to serve, if liked

CAREFULLY SKIN AND GUT THE HARE. Collect all the blood you can into a bowl. Devein the liver if necessary, also cutting out any yellowish bits, and add it to the blood. Cover and chill until needed. Joint the animal, cutting the back into pieces with the help of your strongest knife and a mallet – or make a deal with your friendly local butcher.

Put the pieces of hare in a deep dish and cover with the wine and brandy. Finely chop the garlic and onion, snip the thyme and parsley, and add them all to the marinade, with the bay leaves and peppercorns. Marinate for 24 hours in a cool place.

A few hours before you intend to serve the hare, chop the bacon. Remove the hare from the marinade, drain well, and pat dry with a clean cloth, tea-towel or absorbent paper. Reserve the marinade. Heat the oil and butter in a flameproof casserole or large sauté pan. Put the chopped bacon in the pan, stir over a medium heat for a couple of minutes, then add the hare. Stir for 5–10 minutes until the meat begins to turn brown. Sprinkle in the flour, stir for a minute, then pour in the marinade. Season to taste, stir, cover and cook over a low heat for at least 1 hour, perhaps 2 – the meat is cooked when it begins to come off the bones easily.

Slice the mushrooms and stir them into the pan towards the end of cooking. Remove the reserved liver from the bowl, chop it very finely and stir it into the pan. Simmer for a few more minutes.

Now finish the sauce. Spoon a little of the cooking liquid into the blood to warm it up. Away from the heat, stir it into the sauce until well blended, return to the heat and simmer briskly for 1 minute, stirring all the time – the sauce should be a smooth, dark brown. If you reheat the dish, it will taste just as good though the sauce won't look quite as appealing since it tends to separate. Serve with croûtons, if you like.

BLANQUETTE DE VEAU
Veal in a Cream and Mushroom Sauce

A CLASSIC OF bourgeois cooking, and quite rightly so. Delicate *blanquette* is a dish that does not like to be rushed. After years of producing not unpalatable concoctions that were the colour of milky coffee – unkindly called *brunettes* by the family – I adopted a gentler and more patient approach and, lo, my *blanquettes* turned a grateful shade of white.
Cook *blanquette* on a day you want to relax in your kitchen and serve it with good plain rice and a bowl of small gherkins.

1.2 kg/2¾ lbs breast of veal	Serves 6–8	1½ large lemons
1 carrot		150 g/5 oz button mushrooms
1 large white Spanish onion		45 g/1½ oz/3 tablespoons butter
several sprigs each of thyme and parsley		2 level tablespoons flour
2 bay leaves	sea salt	1–2 large egg yolks
300 ml/½ pint/1¼ cups dry white wine	freshly ground black pepper	120 ml/4 fl oz/½ cup *crème fraîche*
	150 g/5 oz button onions	

TRIM THE BREAST OF VEAL, DISCARDING FAT and sinew as necessary, then cut into 4 cm/1½ in pieces. Soak overnight or for several hours in plenty of fresh cold water. Once the veal has had a good soaking, peel the carrot and cut it into 4 chunks. Quarter the onion. Put the herbs and bay leaves on a small piece of muslin, make into a bag and tie with a string. Drain the veal.

Put the veal with the vegetables and muslin bag in a large heavy-based saucepan. Pour in the wine and add just enough cold water to cover. Over a very moderate heat, bring slowly to a low boil. Conscientiously skim off any scum that may come up to the surface. Season lightly with salt and freshly ground pepper. Reduce the heat a little and simmer *very* gently for 1¼–1½ hours, skimming whenever necessary. The meat should feel tender when you pierce it with a fork at the end of cooking.

Meanwhile, neatly peel the button onions. Blanch them for 5 minutes in lightly salted water. Squeeze the lemons. Trim and slice the mushrooms, then blanch well in boiling water with a dash of lemon juice for a couple of minutes. Drain the onions and mushrooms.

Strain the stock out of the pan into a bowl or jug, leaving the veal in the pan. Discard the muslin bag, then add the drained onions and mushrooms to the pan. Sprinkle with a little lemon juice. Cover to keep warm. If you want to cook the dish in stages, this is a good time to break off. Allow a good half hour to finish off later. And do make sure you reheat everything very gently.

Melt the butter in a saucepan, add the flour and stir for 1 minute to make a very pale roux – do not allow it to colour. Pour the hot stock into the roux, and bring to a boil, stirring vigorously. Simmer gently for a good 10–15 minutes, stirring frequently, the sauce should be smooth and thickened. Now beat the egg yolk or yolks in a bowl, stir in a little hot sauce, then the *crème fraîche*, and beat until thoroughly combined. Pour the mixture into the saucepan, and stir over a low heat. Do not boil.

Pour the sauce over the veal and vegetables. Return to a low heat and stir carefully for a couple of minutes until heated through. Sprinkle in the rest of the lemon juice, check the seasoning, stir and serve immediately.

Veau aux Girolles
Veal with Wild Mushrooms

Mᴀᴋᴇ ᴛʜɪs ᴅɪsʜ with the best mushrooms you feel you can afford. I must admit that I only use little yellow horn-shaped *girolles* (also called *chanterelles*) if I have been lucky enough to be able to gather my own. Otherwise, I use small brown caps.

Serves 6

1.2 kg/2¾ lbs tender veal from the shoulder or leg, tied to make a neat joint

4 baby carrots

4 shallots

2 cloves of garlic

3 tablespoons olive oil

60 g/2 oz/4 tablespoons butter, plus extra to finish

250 ml/8 fl oz/1 cup medium-sweet white wine

sea salt

freshly ground black pepper

750 g/1½ lbs *girolles* or other fragrant mushrooms

2 tablespoons of fresh breadcrumbs

a few sprigs of parsley and chervil

Wɪᴘᴇ ᴀɴᴅ sʟɪᴄᴇ ᴛʜᴇ ᴄᴀʀʀᴏᴛs. Fɪɴᴇʟʏ chop the shallots and crush the garlic. Heat 1 tablespoon of oil and a good knob of butter in a flameproof casserole or sauté pan. Sauté the carrots, shallots and garlic for 1 minute over a very moderate heat, then add the veal joint and sauté until it looks evenly coloured, turning it over gradually.

Moisten with half the wine and a similar amount of water. Season lightly with salt and freshly ground black pepper, then cover tightly.

Reduce the heat and cook very slowly for a good hour. Leave the meat to cool and relax a little. Heat the oven to 200°C/400°F/Gas 6.

Meanwhile, trim and wipe the mushrooms. Heat the rest of the oil in a large frying-pan with a knob of butter. Add the mushrooms and let them sweat for a few minutes over a moderate heat, frequently shaking the pan. Season them with salt and freshly ground black pepper, then drain on absorbent paper. Cut the veal into thin slices. Spread half the mushrooms in a gratin dish. Arrange the slices of veal on top of the mushrooms.

Pour the rest of the wine into the casserole or sauté pan. Stir over a moderately high heat for a minute or two, scraping the bottom of the pan. Sieve the pan juices over the veal. Cover with the rest of the mushrooms. Sprinkle with the breadcrumbs. Snip the herbs over the breadcrumbs, then dot with the rest of the butter. Cook in the oven for 5–10 minutes, until golden, and serve immediately.

CÔTES DE PORC AU CIDRE ET À L'OIGNON
Pan-fried Pork Chops with Onion and Vinegar

A GOOD PAN-FRY to serve with sautéed apple slices, mashed potatoes or *gratin dauphinois* (see page 122).

Serves 4

4 pork chops, not too lean and cut fairly thick

1 clove of garlic

a few sprigs of thyme

4 sage leaves

freshly ground black pepper

60 ml/4 tablespoons/¼ cup medium-dry cider or white wine

1 small onion

1 shallot

olive oil, if needed

3 tablespoons cider or white wine vinegar

3 tablespoons single cream

2 teaspoons mild Dijon mustard

sea salt

CUT THE GARLIC AND RUB THE CHOPS WELL with the cut sides of the garlic. Snip the thyme and sage leaves over the chops, then sprinkle with freshly ground black pepper; rub this seasoning well in on both sides. Cover with cling film and set aside at room temperature for about 1 hour.

Splash the fat around the chops as 2.5 cm/ 1 in intervals. Heat a sauté pan and put the chops in the pan. Cook them over a moderately high heat on both sides for a few minutes, until they turn brown and some fat runs out, then reduce the heat, moisten with the wine or cider and the same amount of water. Cover and cook very gently for 15–20 minutes. Remove the chops from the pan with tongs or a fish slice and keep them warm on a heated serving dish under a heated plate.

Meanwhile, chop the onion and shallot finely. If the chops haven't released much fat, add a little olive oil to the pan juices. Soften the onion and shallot for a few minutes over a moderate heat, stirring frequently. Add the vinegar, scrape the bottom of the pan well, bring to a simmer, then stir in the cream and mustard until hot. Season to taste with salt and a little extra pepper and spoon the sauce over the chops. Serve immediately.

Porc à la Boulangère
Roast Pork with Potatoes

A WEEKEND ROAST after my own heart. Any leftovers will be delicious served with a little garlicky mayonnaise. Use the same method with a leg or shoulder of lamb: it will work just as well.

Serves 6

900 g/2 lbs waxy potatoes

1 large white Spanish onion

oil for greasing

a few sprigs each of parsley and thyme

sea salt

freshly ground black pepper

about 300 ml/½ pint/1¼ cups chicken stock (see page 12), light beef stock or water

60 g/2 oz/4 tablespoons butter

1.4 kg/3 lb loin of pork, boned, trimmed and tied

2–3 cloves of garlic

4 sage leaves

HEAT THE OVEN TO 170°C/325°F/GAS 3. PEEL and slice the potatoes fairly thickly. Thinly slice the onion. Grease a large gratin dish. Spread the sliced potatoes and onion over the bottom of the dish. Snip in the fresh herbs and season lightly with salt and freshly ground black pepper. Pour in just enough stock or water to cover the vegetables. Dot generously with butter and cover with foil. Cook in the oven for about 1 hour.

Now prepare the loin of pork. Cut the garlic and sage leaves into slivers. Using the point of a small sharp knife, make several deep slits into the pork fat and insert the slivers of garlic and sage well into the slits. Rub the loin of pork with a little salt and more generously with

freshly ground black pepper. Set aside at room temperature for about 40 minutes.

Very lightly grease the bottom of a sauté pan. Heat the pan and brown the pork lightly and evenly on all sides over a moderately high heat. Take the potatoes out of the oven, uncover and place the pork on top of the potatoes, replacing the foil before returning to the oven. Turn up the heat to 190°C/375°F/Gas 5 and cook for about 1¼–1½ hours, until the pork is tender and cooked through. Remove the foil for the last 15 minutes.

This dish is best served simply. Leave the pork to relax for a few minutes, then cut it into thin slices and arrange the slices, overlapping slightly, on top of the potatoes.

CASSOULET MAISON
Pork and Haricot Beans Casserole

THIS RECIPE IS relaxed, less fatty than most – and likely to be frowned on by *cassoulet* purists, since I include tomatoes. As I understand it *cassoulet* is a flexible feast. One ingredient that cannot be left out is the *confit* (available from good specialist shops) with its inimitable fat and filamentous texture.
Best prepared a day or two ahead, *cassoulet* makes a splendid *pièce de résistance* for a winter party. Drink with Cahors or Fitou wine. Mop up the juices with good bread and follow with heaps of sharpish green salad.

Serves 12

1 kg/2¼ lbs small white haricot beans

2 large bouquets garnis

2 large onions – 1 stuck with a few cloves

1 large carrot

225 g/8 oz piece gammon or smoked belly of pork

18 cloves of garlic, 12 unpeeled, the rest peeled

12 black peppercorns

225 g/8 oz thick-cut smoked bacon

450 g/1 lb can goose or duck *confit*

450 g/1 lb canned tomatoes

600 ml/1 pint/2½ cups good strong stock

a few sprigs of thyme

1 tablespoon strong Dijon mustard (optional)

few drops chilli or Worcestershire sauce (definitely optional)

small glass brandy (also optional)

12 spicy country sausages (Toulouse or Cumberland)

a small bunch of parsley

90 g/3 oz/1¼ cups white breadcrumbs (day-old bread)

SOAK THE HARICOT BEANS IN PLENTY OF cold water for at least 6 hours. Drain, rinse and bring to the boil in plenty of fresh cold water, with 1 bouquet garni, the clove-studded onion, carrot, piece of gammon or smoked belly of pork, 12 unpeeled garlic cloves and the peppercorns.

Reduce the heat and simmer gently, half-covered, for about 1½ hours until the beans are cooked but still a little firm.

Meanwhile, chop the remaining onion and garlic and the smoked bacon. In a large heavy casserole, brown the onion in a little of the goose or duck fat from the *confit*, and cut up the goose or duck meat into small pieces. Stir the pieces into the browned onion with the chopped bacon and garlic. Add any leg or breast bones to the bean mixture. Cook for a few minutes, stirring, then pour in the tomatoes with their juice and the stock. Add the second bouquet garni, the thyme, and any optional extras. Stir, cover and cook gently for 20–30 minutes. Very slowly grill the sausages until crisp all over and

cooked through, then cut into fork-sized chunks.

Now, to assemble the *cassoulet*. Drain the beans, discard the onion, bones, bouquets garnis and peppercorns. Chop up the carrot and gammon/belly (discarding the fat). If you are going to serve the *cassoulet* in the casserole, transfer the meat stew to a bowl. Ladle a good layer of beans into the casserole. Add half the carrot and gammon/belly, then half the meat stew. Repeat the process, stretching the meat stew with extra hot water if it looks too thick and dry. Top with the remaining beans and the sausages. The *cassoulet* can be put aside at this stage, for up to 24 hours in a cool place.

To finish, snip the parsley into a bowl. Sprinkle the *cassoulet* with the breadcrumbs and parsley, then dot with the remaining duck/ goose fat. About 45–60 minutes before serving heat the oven to 200°C/400°F/Gas 6. Cover the *cassoulet* and heat for 20 minutes, then remove the lid and allow to brown for a further 20 minutes. Serve very hot.

GIGOT
Leg of Lamb

ONE WORD OF caution: you may be disappointed, but I am not going to offer a proper recipe for the greatest of all French festive meat dishes. *Gigot* has to be boldly cooked: there can be few adjustments and no camouflage. And the list of variables to be taken into consideration is more daunting than usual. First there is the lamb itself, and the way it is butchered and prepared. Then comes the roasting tin or dish, and the oven with its own little quirks and tricks. Last but not least, we have the cook, the carver and the guests, with their different hands and palates. And when *gigot* is at stake, in my experience, people always have strong views and great expectations. Quite rightly so. After all, *gigot* is the food of high days and holidays . . .

I HAVE EATEN OTHER PEOPLE'S PERFECT *gigot* and made a quiet note of it. I have on occasion achieved my idea of *gigot* bliss, only to be met by barely polite noises round my table. So rather than a recipe, let me tell you what works for me.

In an ideal world, I will use young Welsh or English lamb, butchered and trimmed French-style, studded with lots of garlic, well seasoned, and rubbed with rosemary and thyme. I would have first discussed the meat with my butcher, then decided whether or not to sit the *gigot* on a few good knobs of butter.

Before I put my *gigot* in the hot oven, I would dribble a little olive oil over it, then cook it very fast, basting a few times with the juices and a trickle of white wine.

Meanwhile, I would plead with the rest of the family, who like their lamb ultra-pink, for the *gigot* to be granted an extra few minutes in the oven, and, hopefully, for injury time afterwards to relax.

In the end I would serve it with *haricots verts* (see page 128), young flageolets (see page 129) and garlic sauce. And for these three items at least I can certainly provide recipes . . .

SAUCE À L'AIL
Garlic Sauce

DON'T BE PUT OFF by the 225 g/8 oz cloves of garlic I use in this recipe. It is not a printing error, and this easy-to-prepare sauce is more aromatic than pungent, because the garlic has been boiled three times. You'll also find that peeling the cooked cloves is a real cinch: simply squeeze them between your thumb and forefinger and they'll just pop out. Garlic sauce is also well worth trying with roast chicken, stuffed with a breadcrumb mixture, particularly if the bird is an ordinary one.

225 g/8 oz cloves of garlic
300 ml/½ pt/1⅓ cups single cream

Serves 6

sea salt
freshly ground black pepper

IN A MEDIUM-SIZED SAUCEPAN BRING the cloves of garlic to the boil in plenty of cold water.

As soon as the water starts bubbling, drain the cloves. Return them to the pan, cover with fresh cold water and bring to the boil again. Drain, then repeat the process one more time.

Now squeeze the softened cloves (see above).

Combine the cream and the peeled cloves in the saucepan and heat through gently until piping hot but not boiling, stirring occasionally.

Liquidise the mixture, season with a little salt and more generously with freshly ground black pepper and serve with *gigot*. This sauce can be reheated if necessary.

AGNEAU EN PAPILLOTE
Marinated Lamb Parcels

A RECIPE I have used and liked for years, from I-am-not-quite-sure where in Provence. I serve this dish with rice, or tiny young flageolets (see page 129) when they are around.

900 g/2 lbs boned shoulder of lamb	Serves 4	a few fennel seeds
1 large ripe tomato		1 bay leaf
1 large unwaxed lemon	a couple of sprigs each of thyme, marjoram, oregano and rosemary	a few mint leaves
5 tablespoons virgin olive oil		freshly ground black pepper
		sea salt

TRIM THE FAT OFF THE MEAT, THEN CUT the shoulder into 12 pieces, not too small but no larger than 4 cm/1½ in. Blanch the tomato in boiling water, then skin it and remove the seeds and pulp. Chop the flesh. Grate and squeeze the lemon.

In a soup plate or shallow bowl, combine the olive oil with the chopped tomato and the grated zest and juice of the lemon. Snip in the herbs. Add a few fennel seeds, then snip in the bay leaf and the mint leaves. Season with freshly ground black pepper. Carefully roll the pieces of lamb in this marinade until they are coated all over. Cover and leave to marinate for 2 hours at room temperature, or longer in the refrigerator.

Heat the oven to 220°C/425°F/Gas 7 with a baking tray. Cut 4 squares of foil, each large enough to comfortably wrap round 3 pieces of lamb. Put 3 pieces of marinated lamb in the centre of each square of foil. Spoon over any remaining marinade. Season with a little salt and extra pepper if you like. Close the parcels, but not too tightly. Put them on the hot baking tray.

Cook for 20–25 minutes and leave the meat to settle for a short while before you open the foil parcels.

110

Navarin d'Agneau
Lamb Stew with Turnips

A TRUSTED LAMB stew. Feel free to vary the vegetables. The turnips are a traditional ingredient, but I sometimes replace them with potatoes, then add leeks and tomatoes half-way through the cooking.

1 kg/2¼ lbs boned lamb
(shoulder or chump)

freshly ground black pepper

1 large white Spanish onion

225 g/8 oz carrots

450 g/1 lb turnips

2–3 cloves of garlic

1 tablespoon oil

2 teaspoons of flour

Serves 6

300 ml/½ pint/1¼ cups light
beef stock or water

100 ml/3½ fl oz/generous ⅓
cup dry white wine

several sprigs of parsley and
rosemary

sea salt

15 g/½ oz/1 tablespoon butter
or 1 tablespoon cream to
finish, if liked

NAVET rouge plat hâtif à feuille entière   82
MAIRÜBEN rote platte   NAVONE rosso piatto
TURNIP Red top   NABO ROJO chato

TRIM A GOOD DEAL OF THE VISIBLE FAT from the meat. Cut it into 5 cm/2 in pieces. Sprinkle the pieces with finely ground black pepper and set aside while you prepare the vegetables. Coarsely chop the onion. Trim and peel the carrots and the turnips and cut them into chunks. Crush the garlic.

Heat the oil in a casserole or large sauté pan. Over a moderately high heat, sauté the meat until lightly coloured, then add the vegetables and sauté for a few minutes, stirring frequently. Sprinkle the flour over the dish and stir to mix it in. Then pour in the stock and the white wine.

Bring the liquid to a simmer, then snip in the herbs and season lightly with salt and freshly ground black pepper. Cover, reduce the heat and cook slowly for about 1½ hours. Skim off the surface fat and scum occasionally.

Once the casserole is cooked, remove the meat and vegetables from the pot with a slotted spoon. Keep them warm. Skim off any fat, then strain the liquid and return it to the pot, turn up the heat and reduce a little. Check the seasoning. Swirl in a knob of butter or a spoonful of cream, if you wish, then return the meat and vegetables to the pot, stir them in well and serve immediately.

TAGINE DE MOUTON YONNÉE
Pot-roasted Lamb with Onions and Raisins

THE PAST IS another country and like everyone else I have always been intrigued by my parents' past, the remote land of before my time. My father and his brothers spent a few happy years as children in North Africa. He returned during the war after escaping from a German POW camp. There he met up with his brother, Jean, and sister-in-law, Yonnée, who were actively working for the Free French. These were dangerous but exciting days, and I have never tired of hearing about them. Many of the North African stories were told around a *couscous* or *tagine*, and over a glass of Boulaouane greyish rosé wine. This recipe of my aunt's is as simple as it is delectable and should be served with rice.

Serves 6

45 g/1½ oz/scant ½ cup raisins

1 cup of cold weak tea

1.2–1.4 kg/2¾–3 lbs shoulder
of mature lamb

3 tablespoons of olive oil

1½ large unwaxed lemons

1 good pinch powdered saffron

1 tablespoon powdered cumin

3 cloves of garlic

sea salt

freshly ground black pepper

900 g/2 lbs large white Spanish
onions

SOAK THE RAISINS IN WEAK TEA OVERNIGHT or for several hours. Trim most of the visible fat from the lamb, then cut it into 5 cm/2 in pieces.

Grease a flameproof casserole with a little olive oil. Grate and squeeze 1 lemon. Put the meat pieces in the casserole, then sprinkle in the lemon juice and zest, the saffron and the cumin. Add the garlic. Season lightly with salt and freshly ground black pepper. Cover and very slowly cook over an extremely low heat for 3 hours.

After about 2½ hours, thinly slice the onions. Heat the rest of the olive oil in a sauté pan and very gently sweat and cook the onions. Stir them frequently and do not allow them to turn brown. Drain the raisins. When the onions are nearly done, stir in the drained raisins.

Add the onions and raisins to the lamb, stir and cook together for a few minutes. Squeeze the remaining half lemon and sprinkle the juice over the dish. Stir and check the seasoning. This dish should be served piping hot.

ROGNONS AU VIN ROUGE
Kidneys in Red Wine

A QUICK AND tasty dish that is good with plain rice.

	Serves 4	
450 g/1 lb lamb's kidneys		sea salt
3 shallots		freshly ground black pepper
1 clove of garlic		grated nutmeg
1 tablespoon oil		2 teaspoons flour
30 g/1 oz/2 tablespoons butter		2 teaspoons mild Dijon mustard
120 ml/4 fl oz/½ cup red wine		2 tablespoons double cream
1 bay leaf		several sprigs of fresh parsley

MAKE THE SAUCE. FINELY CHOP THE SHALlots and garlic. Heat half the oil and a good knob of butter in a heavy-based saucepan. Sweat the shallots and garlic over a low heat until soft, without allowing them to colour. Pour in the red wine and 3 tablespoons of cold water. Add the bay leaf and simmer gently for 5 minutes, stirring occasionally.

Finally, season with a little salt, freshly ground black pepper and a small pinch of grated nutmeg.

While the sauce is cooking, prepare the kidneys. Rinse them well under cold running water, pat dry with absorbent paper and trim off any skin and core. Cut each kidney in half lengthways. Heat the rest of the butter in a frying-pan. Dust the kidneys with flour, then sauté them over a moderately high heat for 3—4 minutes on each side, until they stiffen a little and change colour.

Remove the kidneys from the pan with a slotted spoon and keep warm.

Pour the sauce into the frying-pan, and stir it in thoroughly, scraping up the pan sediments. Add the mustard and the cream, stir in well, then return the kidneys and their juices to the pan. Stir until heated through.

Snip the parsley and sprinkle over the kidneys. To enjoy this dish at its peak, serve immediately.

Bœuf Bourguignon
Beef Cooked in Red Burgundy

Since this dish is infinitely better reheated, I always make it the day before. The last minute addition of brandy, wine and butter, brings the *bourguignon* alive and literally makes the sauce shine.

900 g/2 lbs chuck or blade steak

2 thick-cut rashers rindless smoked streaky bacon

1 large white Spanish onion

1 clove of garlic

1 tablespoon oil

Serves 4

1 tablespoon flour

a few sprigs of thyme

1 bay leaf

1 bottle Burgundy or similar style wine

sea salt

freshly ground black pepper

1 tablespoon brandy

30 g/1 oz/2 tablespoons butter

several sprigs of fresh parsley

Preferably start cooking the dish on the day before you intend to eat it. Trim any surplus fat off the beef. Cut the meat into chunks, not bigger than 5 cm/2 in square. Chop the bacon and onion, and crush the garlic. Heat the oil in a flameproof casserole or large sauté pan. Sauté the chopped bacon until it turns brown. Turn up the heat a little, add the beef and brown quickly on all sides.

Remove the meat from the pan with a slotted spoon. Add the onion and sauté until it colours. Return the meat to the pan, add the garlic and sprinkle with the flour. Stir for a couple of minutes, then add the thyme, bay leaf and three-quarters of the bottle of wine. Season with a little salt, more generously with freshly ground black pepper, and bring to a simmer, stirring occasionally.

Now reduce the heat to very low, cover tightly and cook extremely slowly for at least 2½ hours, giving the mixture an occasional stir. Turn off the heat and leave overnight to mature.

The next day, very gently reheat the dish for about 40 minutes. Take out the meat with tongs or a slotted spoon and put it on a plate, or if you prefer, pile it on a serving dish. Turn up the heat a little, stir in the brandy and cook for a few minutes.

Meanwhile, snip the parsley. Pour the rest of the wine into the pan, swirl in the butter, stir, then either return the meat to the pan or pour the sauce over the meat in the serving dish.

Sprinkle with the parsley and serve immediately.

Bœuf en Daube
Slow-cooked Beef Casserole

ONE OF MY favourite of French country casseroles, and very different in texture and flavour. Unlike *bœuf bourguignon*, this dish is best served with rice or pasta rather than potatoes.

1 kg/2¼ lbs braising steak

1 large white Spanish onion

1 shallot

2 bay leaves

several sprigs each of thyme and parsley

a few black peppercorns

Serves 5–6

3 tablespoons olive oil

about 550 ml/18 fl oz/2⅓ cups light red wine

4 thick-cut rashers of rindless smoked streaky bacon

2 cloves of garlic

2 large ripe tomatoes

12 black olives

200 g/7 oz mushrooms

sea salt

freshly ground black pepper

TRIM ANY VISIBLE FAT OFF THE MEAT, THEN cut into 5 cm/2 in chunks. Chop the onion and shallot. In a large bowl, combine the meat, onion and shallot, bay leaves, thyme, parsley and peppercorns with half the oil and just enough red wine to cover. Leave to marinate overnight.

The next day, heat the oven to 170°C/325°F/ Gas 3. Chop the bacon. In a flameproof casserole dish, heat the rest of the oil, add the bacon and sauté until it begins to brown. Take the meat out of the marinade, reserving the marinade. Drain well, and pat dry with a clean cloth or absorbent paper. Add the meat to the dish and brown on all sides for a few minutes over a moderately high heat.

Coarsely chop the garlic and tomatoes. Stone and chop the olives, and wipe and slice the mushrooms. Add all these to the dish together with the onion and shallot from the marinade. Stir well.

Cover the dish tightly and cook in the oven for 20 minutes. Take the dish out of the oven. Pour in the reserved marinade. Season to taste with salt and freshly ground black pepper. Stir thoroughly, cover the dish tightly again, and return to the oven.

Turn the oven down low. Cook for a good 3 hours, occasionally checking to see that there is still enough wine to come halfway up the pieces of meat. Add a little extra wine if necessary.

Serve hot.

POT AU FEU
Boiled Beef with Vegetables

THE GRAND OLD one-pot meal of France – and
a good way to make a proper light beef stock. In my experience, there is never a great deal of left-over beef,
but what there may be is excellent served cold with a garlicky mayonnaise.
There never seems to be enough marrow either. When I was a child, the precious substance was always
ceremoniously given on a piece of toast to my grandmother, while we all wondered what on earth the
fuss was about . . .

1 kg/2¼ lbs lean braising beef	Serves 8	several sprigs each of chervil and parsley
1 kg/2¼ lbs shin of beef, meat and bone		freshly ground black pepper
1 large marrow bone		TO SERVE
3 cloves of garlic	4 medium-sized potatoes	strong Dijon mustard
2 bay leaves	8 button onions	coarse grain mustard
several sprigs of thyme	4 large leeks	coarse sea salt
6 carrots	4 stalks of celery	gherkins
4 turnips	sea salt	creamed horseradish

INTO YOUR LARGEST HEAVY-BASED SAUCEPAN
or stockpot, put the meat bones. Trim off most
of the visible fat, then cut the meat into large
pieces – no smaller than about 7.5 cm/3 in
square – and tie them together. Put the meat on
top of the bones. Cover with plenty of cold
water, add the garlic, bay leaves and thyme,
and very slowly bring to the boil over an
extremely low heat. Skim off any greyish scum
as soon as it comes up to the surface.

While the meat is coming to the boil,
carefully prepare the vegetables. Peel the
carrots and cut them into segments. Peel the
turnips and cut in half, or quarter them if they
are large. Peel the potatoes and cut in half. Peel
the onions neatly. Trim the leeks, cut in half
lengthways and rinse them well. Trim and
rinse the stalks of celery. Tie together the leeks
and celery into 3 parcels.

Add the carrots, turnips and potatoes to the
pan. Bring back to a very gentle boil and skim
off any scum. Season lightly with salt. Now add

the onions and the leek and celery parcels.
Bring back to a low boil, skim again and partly
cover. Cook very slowly for at least another 2½
hours, skimming until any foam that comes up
looks light and white. Add the parsley and
chervil after 1 hour or so.

Take off the heat and leave to settle for a few
minutes. Remove any surface fat with a spoon.
Lift out the meat and vegetables with a slotted
spoon. Discard the strings, then heap meat and
vegetables attractively on a serving dish. Spoon
out the marrow and reserve for your most
honoured or senior guest. Discard the bones.

Strain the stock through a sieve lined with a
muslin or clean fine cloth into a saucepan.
Bring to a simmer, add a little freshly ground
black pepper, and salt if necessary, then
moisten the meat and vegetables with a little
sauce. Pour some more stock into a bowl to
serve with the dish. Have on the table at the
same time different kinds of mustards, coarse
sea salt and creamed horseradish.

BŒUF MODE
Braised Beef

Bœuf mode can be served hot, or cold which I much prefer. It makes a splendid party dish.

Serves 8

1 calf's foot, split in half

4 thick-cut rashers of smoked back bacon

1.8 kg/4 lbs rolled topside of beef, larded and barded

300 ml/½ pint/1¼ cups dry white wine, plus extra, if needed

2 cloves of garlic

several sprigs of parsley and thyme

2–3 bay leaves

sea salt

freshly ground black pepper

about 24 button onions

450 g/1 lb baby carrots

Rinse and scrub the calf's foot, then blanch it for a few minutes in boiling water. Drain, and cut into pieces (if you wish – and possess a cleaver or heavy knife). Chop the bacon.

Place a large flameproof casserole over a moderate heat. Add the chopped bacon to the dish and sauté until the juices begin to run. Add the beef and brown lightly and evenly on all sides. Now add the calf's foot, and moisten with the white wine and about the same quantity of water. Chop or crush the garlic and add to the dish with the sprigs of herbs and the bay leaves. Season lightly with salt and freshly ground black pepper. Cover tightly and cook over a very low heat for a good 2 hours.

After about 2 hours, peel and trim the onions. Scrape the baby carrots and cut into segments. Add the onions and carrots to the pan, with a little extra wine and water if the level of the liquid looks too low. Cover and cook for a further 1½ hours, over a low heat.

If you want to eat this dish hot, leave off the heat for at least 10 minutes. Skim the fat off the surface before serving. Chill any remains: the jellied leftovers will be excellent served cold the following day.

To serve the whole dish cold, allow the beef to cool in the casserole until barely warm. Remove it from the pot and leave to get cold on a large plate, then cover it with foil and chill for a couple of hours. Strain the liquid – reserving the vegetables and the pieces of calf's foot. Leave the liquid to get cold and then chill. Also refrigerate the vegetables and calf's foot.

Remove the strings and the outer fat from the chilled beef and cut it into thin slices. Arrange the slices on a large serving dish, so that they overlap attractively. Surround with the reserved vegetables and pieces of calf's foot. Spoon the jellied or syrupy sauce over the lot, and sprinkle very lightly with freshly ground black pepper. Cover the dish with cling film or foil and chill until ready to serve.

STEAKS AU POIVRE ET AUX ANCHOIS
Steaks with Pepper and Anchovy

ONE OF MY favourite 'quickie' sauces. My husband is more of a steak-eater than I and he believes in warming the steaks in a little butter before patting in the crushed peppercorns. It does seem to deepen the peppery flavour but, since he got the idea from a James Beard book and is English anyway, I am only mentioning this as an aside and for the sake of *entente cordiale* and *matrimoniale*.

Serves 4

4 steaks, from the fillet or
rump, about 4 cm/1½ in thick

2 level tablespoons black
peppercorns

1 tablespoon oil

60 g/2 oz/4 tablespoons butter

2 tablespoons dry white wine

3 tablespoons *crème fraîche* or
double cream

2 teaspoons anchovy paste

1 tablespoon brandy

AT LEAST 1 HOUR BEFORE YOU WANT TO start cooking the steaks, crush the peppercorns with the help of a pestle and mortar. Sprinkle the crushed peppercorns over the steaks, then press them in firmly with your hands. Cover with cling film and set aside at room temperature.

In a large heavy-based frying-pan, heat the oil and a good knob of butter over a high heat. Cut the rest of the butter into small pieces. Add the steaks and cook for 2–4 minutes on each side, depending on your taste and the thickness, and cut, of the meat.

Put the steaks on a hot serving dish. Now swirl the wine into the pan, stir it for a minute, scraping the bottom of the pan, then add the cream and anchovy paste. Stir until heated through, then swirl in the brandy. Away from the heat, swirl in the pieces of butter. Pour the sauce over the steaks and serve at once.

HACHIS PARMENTIER
French Cottage Pie

THERE IS ABSOLUTELY no reason to turn up one's nose (however refined) at left-over beef when it is done this way. Having said that, I must admit that bland *hachis parmentier*, thriftily made from plain minced cooked beef and thin potato purée, is a pretty mean concoction. The one we did at home wasn't particularly economical, but it did taste good. And quite often I much preferred it to the roast it originated from . . .

	Serves 4–5	
2 thick-cut rashers of rindless smoked streaky bacon		a dash of Worcestershire sauce
		a dash of tomato ketchup
1 smallish onion	60 ml/4 tablespoons/¼ cup red wine	350 g/12 oz not too heavy *purée de pommes de terre* (see page 123)
2 shallots		
1 clove of garlic	sea salt	45 g/1½ oz Gruyère
1 tablespoon olive oil	freshly ground black pepper	45 g/1½ oz/generous ½ cup breadcrumbs (day-old bread)
60 g/2 oz/4 tablespoons butter	a pinch of cayenne pepper or chilli powder, if liked	
about 350 g/12 oz cooked beef		

BRIEFLY WHIZZ TOGETHER THE BACON, onion, shallots and garlic in a food processor. Heat the oil with a knob of butter in a frying-pan. Brown the bacon, onion and garlic mixture over a fairly high heat. Meanwhile, quickly process the cooked beef. Add the beef to the pan, stir in well and sauté for a couple of minutes, still over a fairly high heat. Heat the oven to 230°C/450 °F/Gas 8.

Pour the wine into the frying-pan and season to taste with salt and freshly ground black pepper. Add a little cayenne or chilli, if liked,

and a dash of Worcestershire sauce and ketchup. Reduce the heat a little and simmer for 10 minutes, stirring occasionally.

Butter a gratin dish. Spread a thin layer of creamed potato over the bottom of the dish. Cover with the beef hash spreading it evenly. Cover with the rest of the creamed potato. Grate the Gruyère over the dish and sprinkle with the breadcrumbs. Dot with the rest of the butter.

Bake for 15 minutes until the topping is golden brown. Serve immediately, piping hot.

GRATIN DAUPHINOIS/*Potato Gratin*

PURÉE DE POMMES DE TERRE MARTHE
Creamed Potatoes

POMMES DE TERRE SAUTÉES TATA BOUCHER
Sautéed Potatoes

POIREAUX À LA CRÈME/*Leeks with Cream*

PETITS POIS À LA LAITUE ET AUX PETITS OIGNONS
Baby Peas with Lettuce and Onions

CAROTTES AU CUMIN
Carrots Cooked with Cumin

RATATOUILLE
Ragoût of Provençal Vegetables

GRATIN D'AUBERGINES/*Aubergine Gratin*

PURÉE D'OIGNONS/*Onion Purée*

HARICOTS VERTS FOURCHETTES
French Beans

FLAGEOLETS AU NATUREL
Simple Flageolet Beans

HARICOTS EN BOÎTE AMÉLIORÉS
Improved Canned Haricot Beans

CHAMPIGNONS FARCIS/*Stuffed Mushrooms*

CHAMPIGNONS À LA POÊLE
Pan-fried Mushrooms

TOMATES FARCIES BIJOU
Herb-stuffed Tomatoes

POMMES DE TERRE À LA FORESTIÈRE
Sautéed Potatoes with Mushrooms and Bacon

LENTILLES AUX LARDONS
Lentils with Bacon

ENDIVES AU FOUR/*Baked Chicory*

Légumes

Vegetables

Whenever they come back from a holiday in France, my English and American vegetarian friends are always quick to point out that they find eating in the average French restaurant rather a depressing experience.

They explain vividly that there are very few vegetables on menus – never mind vegetarian dishes. I make patriotic excuses, of course, but to some extent I sympathise with them. A couple of years ago, travelling around the Toulouse – Albi region and eating in restaurants that the locals treated as their canteens, I soon wondered where all the vegetables were. This was September and the markets were bursting with vivid colours and mellow produce. But here we were, everywhere we went, being offered five-course menus that were incredibly high on value and animal protein. Withdrawal symptoms soon set in and I got to munching tomatoes in the car. After a few days, when we got to Cahors, I was overwhelmed with joy to discover that it had one vegetarian restaurant. It was tucked away near the cathedral, a throw-back to the Seventies in its treatment of nut rissoles and general décor. But, how wonderful, at last, to be able to savour a meal built on the wealth of vegetables I had admired on the markets.

To eat vegetables in France, you have to go to someone's home. Depending on whether it is lunch or dinner, you'll begin the meal with crudités or soup, probably have potatoes or maybe plain rice or pasta with the main course, then almost certainly a green salad. A separate vegetable course is a strong possibility in the evening, particularly if the meal does not include meat. In fact, provided they eat eggs as well, I think my vegetarian friends would quite enjoy supper in a French home.

GRATIN DAUPHINOIS
Potato Gratin

D*AUPHINOIS*, THE GREATEST *gratin* of them all, is a traditional accompaniment to roasts. In my opinion, at its creamy luxurious best, it deserves to be a course in its own right.

Gratin dauphinois is another of those dishes that no two people will ever make exactly the same. Mado, my grandmother's cook, first taught me a *gratin* made with thick-cut potatoes, milk, no eggs, and good knobs of butter. My mother preferred thick slices of potato, 2 eggs and a mixture of milk and *crème fraîche*. I now find that if I am using cream, the *gratin* works better with thin slices, and if milk, thick slices . . . Ah well. One egg yolk does help though, and the good thing is, you can't really go wrong anyway.

Serves 6–8

900 g/2 lbs large waxy potatoes

2–3 cloves of garlic

butter

550 ml/18 fl oz/2⅓ cups full-fat milk, or 450 ml/¾ pint/2 cups single cream or a mixture of the two

1–2 egg yolks

a pinch of grated nutmeg

sea salt

freshly ground black pepper

HEAT THE OVEN TO 170°C/325°F/GAS 3. PEEL the potatoes and slice them evenly – I do this with the slicing disc of the food processor. Cut the cloves of garlic. Rub a gratin dish thoroughly with the cut sides of the cloves, then crush the garlic. Generously grease the dish with butter.

Gently warm the milk, cream or mixture of both in a saucepan. Whisk in the egg yolks and stir in a pinch of nutmeg. Season with a little salt and freshly ground black pepper.

Spread a layer of potatoes in the prepared dish. Scatter over some of the crushed garlic.

Season lightly. Spoon or trickle in a little of the milk or cream mixture. Repeat until all the potatoes are used up, ending with a good layer of milk or cream. Dot the surface with several little knobs of butter.

Cook in the oven for 1 hour, then turn up the heat to 200°C/400°F/Gas 6, and cook for another 20–30 minutes, until the *gratin* is golden brown and the potatoes tender. This you can test with a skewer.

If the potatoes aren't quite done, reduce the heat to the original setting and cook for a further 15 minutes.

Purée de Pommes de Terre Marthe
Creamed Potatoes

Marthe was our daily in Paris and quite a character. She had left school at 12, but she wrote well-turned sentences in a fine hand and could be relied on to advise us on grammar. She wore dentures which fascinated us, and she had a strange habit of piecing together torn up letters from wastepaper baskets. One day she confronted my father with one such discarded message. She was livid. How *could* Monsieur . . . Monsieur had so hated the Camembert at supper the previous evening that he had written a sarcastic note to Marthe to that effect (he always left for work before she arrived and was, and is, a great memo writer). Naturally he had soon thought better of it and torn up the note. He should have used a shredder: it took him – and my mother – a long time to pacify Marthe. We girls sided with her. How could anyone be so cruel, even if he changed his mind later . . .

Marthe made the best creamed potatoes I have ever tasted, deceptively light and totally irresistible. This is more or less her recipe – rather less than more, because I use just a little less egg and butter.

1.1 kg/2½ lbs waxy potatoes	Serves 6–8	60 g/2 oz/4 tablespoons butter, plus extra to finish, if liked
sea salt		1 egg yolk
250 ml/8 fl oz/1 cup milk		freshly ground black pepper

Bring a large saucepan of lightly salted water to the boil. Peel the potatoes and cut them in half, or quarters if they are very large. Add the potatoes to the boiling water. Bring back to the boil, reduce the heat a little and simmer gently until the potatoes are cooked but not mushy. Do not let the water bubble too fast, or the potatoes will cook unevenly and disintegrate.

Meanwhile, heat the milk in a small saucepan until very hot but not quite boiling. Drain the potatoes well. Pass them through a *mouli* or mash lightly with a potato masher. Return the potatoes to the pan, with the butter, and stir gently over a low heat to remove the excess moisture.

Whisk in the hot milk a little at a time, working vigorously. Beat the egg into the last few spoonfuls of milk, and whisk this into the potatoes. Season to taste. If you like, swirl in a good knob of butter. Serve at once.

The purée should not really be reheated (except when making *hachis parmentier*, page 119). But it will keep warm for up to 15 minutes in a bowl, covered with a heated plate, set over a pan of very hot water.

Pommes de Terre Sautées Tata Boucher
Sautéed Potatoes

I HAVE ALREADY mentioned Madame Boucher, she of the magnificent omelettes. Her sautéed potatoes were equally satisfying. Perhaps this is why in our gratefulness we dubbed her Tata: although not our aunt or great-aunt, she is an honorary and honoured member of the family.

	Serves 6	
1 kg/2¼ lbs waxy potatoes		sea salt
5 tablespoons oil		freshly ground black pepper
45 g/1½ oz/3 tablespoons butter		several sprigs of parsley

PEEL THE POTATOES AND CUT THEM INTO rough small dice, about 2 cm/¾ in and certainly no larger than 2.5 cm/1 in. Rinse the diced potatoes in hot water, drain well and dry them thoroughly with a clean cloth or absorbent paper – this seems to prevent the potatoes from sticking together during cooking.

In a very large heavy-based frying-pan, heat the oil and butter. Add the potatoes – the pan should be large enough to take them very comfortably more or less in a single layer. Otherwise use 2 pans.

Season liberally with salt and pepper. Over a low heat sauté the potatoes until they are crisp and golden. Be patient, because this may take up to 1 hour. Turn the heat down a little if the potatoes are browning too much. Stir frequently with a wooden spatula and give the pan a good shake every now and then. Towards the end of cooking, snip the parsley into a bowl.

You shouldn't need to drain the potatoes on absorbent paper, but do so if they look remotely greasy. Check the seasoning, sprinkle the potatoes with the snipped parsley and serve.

Poireaux à la Crème
Leeks with Cream

THIS IS A good vegetable dish to bear in mind if you know you are going to be pushed for time at the last minute. The softened leeks will happily keep for several hours. Reheat and finish off just before serving.

	Serves 6	
1 kg/2¼ lbs leeks		freshly ground black pepper
60 g/2 oz/4 tablespoons butter		1 egg yolk
sea salt		2–3 tablespoons *crème fraîche* or soured cream

TRIM THE LEEKS. SLIT THEM LENGTHWAYS and wash them thoroughly in cold water. Drain well, dry with a clean cloth or absorbent paper, then chop them.

Heat the butter in a sauté pan, then sauté the leeks until soft over a moderately low heat, stirring frequently. Season to taste with salt and freshly ground black pepper. Combine the egg yolk and *crème fraîche* or soured cream. Stir into the leeks. Season to taste and serve hot.

Petits Pois à la Laitue et aux Petits Oignons
Baby Peas with Lettuce and Onions

Fresh from the garden, *petits pois* have always been one of the joys of the summer table. I sometimes add one or two chopped rashers of green bacon to the other ingredients at the beginning of the recipe.

Serves 4

2 kg/4½ lbs unshelled, or 500 g /1 lb 2 oz shelled baby peas

60 g/2 oz/4 tablespoons butter

2 tender lettuces

1 medium-sized mild onion, or 2 small onions

150 ml/¼ pint/⅔ cup light chicken stock or water

1 teaspoon sugar

sea salt

freshly ground black pepper

Shell the peas. Melt the butter in a heavy-based saucepan. Wash and coarsely shred the lettuces. Peel and very thinly slice the onion or onions. Add the peas, lettuces and onion to the pan. Stir to coat in butter, then cover. Cook very gently over a low heat for 5–10 minutes, shaking the pan occasionally.

Add the stock or cold water, and sprinkle in the sugar. Season with a little salt and freshly ground black pepper.

Cover and cook over a low heat for 15–20 minutes until the peas are tender. Taste, and adjust the seasoning. Then drain and serve immediately.

Carottes au Cumin
Carrots Cooked with Cumin

A good way to cook mature carrots.

Serves 6

1.2 kg/2¾ lbs carrots

2–3 tablespoons olive oil

sea salt

freshly ground black pepper

1–2 cloves garlic

1 teaspoon ground cumin

3 tablespoons white wine

Peel and slice the carrots. Heat the oil in a sauté pan. Add the carrots, season lightly with salt and freshly ground black pepper and cook over a low heat for about 15 minutes, stirring occasionally.

Crush the garlic and add to the pan with the cumin. Stir well, then moisten with the white wine and a glass of water. Cover and cook very gently for 45 minutes, shaking the pan from time to time. Drain and serve hot.

RATATOUILLE
Ragoût of Provençal Vegetables

RATATOUILLE TASTES BEST in late summer when vegetables are at their peak of ripeness. There is a painstaking way of making *ratatouille*, which involves sautéing the vegetables separately before the final assembly. It produces an excellent *ratatouille*, but it takes infinitely longer than the recipe below. And somehow I don't think the end result justifies the effort. I prefer this slightly coarser version. If nothing else, it is closer in spirit to the name of the dish: *touiller* is a slangy way of saying stir or mix. As for *rata*, any French conscript will tell you that it just means plain old army grub.

Ratatouille is particularly good served with a plain omelette.

Serves 4–6

2 medium-sized aubergines

3 cloves of garlic

6 tablespoons olive oil

2 sweet red peppers

1 large white onion

6 small courgettes

2 large ripe tomatoes

a few sprigs of thyme, sweet savoury, marjoram and oregano

sea salt

freshly ground black pepper

several sprigs of parsley

PEEL THE AUBERGINES AND CUT THEM crossways into thin slices. Cut one of the cloves of garlic and use it to rub a wide heavy-based saucepan or sauté pan. Crush the rest of the garlic.

Heat 2 tablespoons of olive oil in the pan. Sauté the sliced aubergines for a few minutes.

Meanwhile, core and thinly slice the peppers. Add the peppers to the pan and sauté gently for a few minutes, until softening. Take care not to overcook them.

Slice the onion very thinly. Add another tablespoon of olive oil to the pan then stir in the onion rings. Sauté for a few minutes, stirring occasionally.

Meanwhile, cut the courgettes, then blanch, peel, seed and chop the tomatoes. Stir the courgettes into the pan. Sauté for a couple of minutes, then add the chopped tomatoes and the crushed garlic. Snip in the thyme, sweet savoury, marjoram and oregano. Season lightly with salt and freshly ground black pepper. Stir in another 2 tablespoons of olive oil and cover the pan. Reduce the heat a little and cook very gently for 30–40 minutes, stirring occasionally.

Snip in the parsley and add one more tablespoon of olive oil. Continue cooking on a low heat for 5–10 minutes. Check the seasoning. Serve hot, warm, or cold, as you prefer.

GRATIN D'AUBERGINES
Aubergine Gratin

From the family's summer repertoire, a dish that seduced my elders on the island of Porquerolles, off the Lavandou coast, between Toulon and St Tropez.
I often leave out the Gruyère in order to enjoy the full Mediterranean flavours of the vegetables, but Gruyère featured in the original recipe and so stays in as an option. Either way, this is a good dish to serve to vegetarians.

	Serves 6	
3–4 unblemished large, long aubergines		a few sprigs of marjoram and oregano
olive oil		1–2 teaspoons sugar
750 g/1½ lbs ripe tomatoes		sea salt
2–3 cloves of garlic		freshly ground black pepper
several sprigs each of parsley, thyme and chervil		150 g/5 oz Gruyère, if liked

Wipe the aubergines. Slice them thinly lengthways without peeling. Heat 1 tablespoon of olive oil in a large frying-pan. Sauté the aubergine slices over a moderate heat, a few at a time. Turn them over as soon as they become a little crisp and golden on the underside. Drain them well on a thick layer of absorbent paper, turning them over to mop up as much fat as possible.

Continue in the same way until all the aubergines are sautéed, adding more oil as necessary. Turn down the heat a little after awhile and resist any impulse to speed up the process – aubergines burn all too readily. At the same time blanch the tomatoes in boiling water, then peel, cut in half, remove the seeds and chop the flesh coarsely.

Crush the garlic. In a sauté pan, heat 1 tablespoon of olive oil. Tip in the tomatoes. Add the crushed garlic, snip in the herbs and sprinkle in the sugar. Cook over a low heat until the mixture becomes a soft purée, stirring frequently. Season with a little salt and freshly ground black pepper. Heat the oven to 180°C/350°F/Gas 4. Grate the Gruyère, if using.

Put a layer of aubergine slices in the bottom of a gratin dish. Season lightly. Spread a thin layer of tomato purée over the aubergines. If you are using Gruyère, sprinkle a little on top of the tomatoes. Repeat until all the ingredients are used up. Sprinkle the top layer with a little olive oil. Cook in the oven for a good hour. Eat warm rather than hot, and preferably as a separate course.

Purée d'Oignons
Onion Purée

This side-dish nicely accompanies plain roasts, grills and pan-fries. It can be made well ahead and reheated at the last minute. I sometimes add a few cloves of garlic to the onions.

30 g/1 oz/¼ cup raisins
200 ml/8 fl oz hot weak tea
500 g/1 lb 2 oz onions
30 g/1 oz/2 tablespoons butter
2 tablespoons sugar

Serves 6

90 ml/3 fl oz/⅓ cup dry white wine
3 tablespoons white wine vinegar
sea salt
freshly ground black pepper

Soak the raisins in the tea. Meanwhile, coarsely chop the onions. Melt the butter in a saucepan. Over a low heat, gently sweat the onions in the butter, without letting them brown. Sprinkle in the sugar, stir and cover. Reduce the heat to very low. Cover and cook for 15 minutes, occasionally shaking the pan.

Now add the wine, stir, cover and cook for another 15 minutes, still very gently. Stir in the vinegar and continue cooking for 10 minutes. Drain the raisins, add them to the pan, season lightly and cook for a further 15 minutes. The onions will be meltingly soft and only lightly coloured. Serve hot.

Haricots Verts Fourchettes
French Beans

On summer evenings, at my grandparents' house, we have often consumed vast platters of beans prepared this way. The exact amount of butter, garlic and parsley varies with the cook. The quantities below are a moderate guideline.

500 g/1 lb 2 oz young French green beans
sea salt
1 small clove of garlic

Serves 4

several sprigs of parsley
45 g/1½ oz/3 tablespoons butter
freshly ground black pepper

Top and tail the beans and remove any strings. Bring a large saucepan of water to the boil. Add a little salt. Throw in the beans, bring back to the boil and keep the water bubbling away until the beans are cooked to your liking, but preferably still a little firm. While the beans are cooking, crush the garlic, and snip the parsley into a bowl.

Have a big bowl of iced water ready. Quickly drain the beans and plunge into the iced water. Leave them in for a few seconds and drain again. Dry in a clean cloth if you like. Now melt the butter in a sauté pan. Add the well-drained beans to the butter with the garlic and parsley. Mix well, stir over a moderate heat and serve when heated through.

FLAGEOLETS AU NATUREL
Simple Flageolet Beans

A DISH I ONLY do when I see really attractive fresh-looking small flageolets, sometimes at my local health food store in London but more likely on a French market in the autumn. The rest of the time I am content enough with my cans (see page 130).

Ideal with *gigot* and good with duck, these flageolets (without the butter finish) also make the basis of a good salad. Dress with olive oil and lemon juice, add plenty of snipped spring onions, chives and parsley, then serve at room temperature.

500 g/1 lb 2 oz young flageolet beans	Serves 4–6	1.5 l/2½ pints/6 cups liquid made up from chicken stock and water
a few sprigs each of thyme and marjoram		sea salt
3 sage leaves		freshly ground black pepper
1 bay leaf		45 g/1½ oz/3 tablespoons butter
1 clove of garlic		several sprigs of fresh parsley

SOAK THE FLAGEOLETS FOR 1–2 HOURS – the fresher they are, the less they will need to soak. Discard any damaged beans that may have come up to the surface. Drain and rinse.

Place the herbs and the garlic on a piece of muslin. Form the muslin into a little pouch, and secure it with fine string. Into a large heavy-based saucepan, pour the chicken stock and water. Add the flageolets and the muslin pouch.

Bring slowly to the boil, skim off any scum, then cover and simmer gently for 40 minutes. Season with salt and freshly ground black pepper. Cover again and continue to simmer gently until the flageolets are cooked and soft, skimming occasionally. This will probably take another 30 minutes at least. The exact timing will depend on the freshness and quality of the flageolets.

When the flageolets are cooked, drain them well. Swirl in the butter and snip in the parsley before serving.

Haricots en Boîte Améliorés
Improved Canned Haricot Beans

I WAS BROUGHT up not to have any qualms about using canned haricot and flageolet beans. Look out for *flageolets extra fins* in particular. They are worth stocking up on, and excellent with lamb, sausages or bacon.

450 g/1 lb can of flageolets or haricot beans

1 clove of garlic

1 large white Spanish onion or several button onions

Serves 4

1 large ripe tomato

1 tablespoon olive oil

1 tablespoon butter

sea salt

freshly ground black pepper

DRAIN AND COPIOUSLY RINSE THE CANNED beans. Finely chop the garlic and the large onion, if using. If using button onions, blanch them for several minutes in boiling water. Drain well. Blanch the tomato, then peel, seed and chop it.

Heat the olive oil in a sauté pan. Add the garlic, prepared onion or button onions, and tomato. Sauté gently for a few minutes, until softened. Add the drained beans and 6 tablespoons of water. Heat through gently over a low heat, stirring lightly a few times.

Drain. Tip into a serving dish, then swirl in the butter and season to taste. Serve hot.

Champignons Farcis
Stuffed Mushrooms

A GUTSY AND buttery dish worth serving as a separate course.

Serves 4

4 very large or 8 medium-sized undamaged flat mushrooms

olive oil and butter for greasing

FOR THE STUFFING

120 g/4 oz/8 tablespoons butter

2 canned anchovy fillets or 2 teaspoons anchovy paste

2–3 cloves of garlic

several sprigs each of parsley and chives

45 g/1½ oz/generous ½ cup breadcrumbs, made from day-old bread

sea salt

freshly ground black pepper

HEAT THE OVEN TO 190°C/375°F/GAS 5. WIPE the mushrooms. Break or cut off the stalks. Trim off the gritty bottom ends, then finely chop the rest of the stalks and reserve. Use either individual round gratin dishes or a large dish. Grease well first with oil, then with butter.

Prepare the stuffing. Quickly whizz together the butter, chopped mushroom stalks, anchovy fillets (drained of their oil) or anchovy paste, garlic, parsley and chives, and breadcrumbs in a food processor. Using a palette knife, spread the stuffing over the mushroom caps. Season lightly with salt and more generously with freshly ground black pepper.

Arrange the mushrooms on the gratin dishes or dish. Bake for 30–40 minutes, until the mushrooms are soft and the stuffing golden and sizzling.

Serve hot.

CHAMPIGNONS À LA POÊLE
Pan-fried Mushrooms

OYSTER MUSHROOMS ARE called *pleurotes* in French (from a Greek word for 'little ear'). Whether they look to you and me like bivalves or ears, both names are charmingly appropriate. On a recent visit to a mushroom farm, I saw them growing commercially in a constantly lit cellar for the first time. Here they were, in fact, very mussel rather than oyster-like, in clusters on a wall of well-insulated manure.

The owner of the place enjoyed hearing about their English name. *Très amusant, mais* . . . Before I could add pedantically that their French name was very apt too, she told me just why *pleurotes* are called *pleurotes*. These mushrooms, she explained, give of their best if you cook them briefly in a little hot fat, then let them weep (*pleurer*) awhile before you finish the cooking. And that, Madame, is how they got their name.

Serves 6

225 g/8 oz oyster mushrooms

1 tablespoon oil

60 g/2 oz/4 tablespoons butter

sea salt

450 g/1 lb brown cap
mushrooms

2–3 cloves of garlic

several sprigs of parsley

freshly ground black pepper

1 lemon wedge, if liked

a few sprigs of chives, if liked

HEAT THE OIL AND A KNOB OF BUTTER IN a large frying-pan. Break the oyster mushrooms if they look unwieldy. Sauté the oyster mushrooms over a moderately high heat for a few minutes, stirring frequently. Season with a little salt. Remove the mushrooms from the pan with a slotted spoon, and spread them over a double layer of absorbent paper. Reduce the heat and add the rest of the butter to the pan.

Trim the brown caps, and cut them in half, or quarters if they are on the large side. Crush the garlic. Put the brown caps and garlic in the pan, stir to coat in the melted butter. Season with a little salt. Turn up the heat just a notch and sauté the mushrooms for several minutes, until they are nearly cooked to your liking.

Stir in the reserved oyster mushrooms. Snip in the parsley and sauté for a couple of minutes, stirring frequently. Season to taste. If wished, sprinkle with a little lemon juice and snip in some chives just before serving.

Tomates Farcies Bijou
Herb-stuffed Tomatoes

My mother's way of stuffing tomatoes – perfect if you have access to a summer garden, and also not bad with dried herbs. Particularly recommended with roast lamb and chicken dishes.

8 firm but ripe, medium-sized tomatoes	Serves 4	a few sprigs of as many of the following as you like: sweet savory, thyme, oregano and marjoram
sea salt		
1–2 cloves of garlic		1 teaspoon sugar, if liked
3 tablespoons good olive oil		30 g/1 oz/2 tablespoons butter
2 tablespoons breadcrumbs made with day-old bread	several sprigs each of parsley, chervil, chives and tarragon	freshly ground black pepper

Slice off the tops of the tomatoes. Using a small sharp knife and a teaspoon, carefully remove the seeds and pulp. Sprinkle the tomatoes with a little salt. Place them upside down on absorbent paper and leave to drain for at least 20 minutes. Heat the oven to 180°C/350°F/Gas 4.

Very finely chop the garlic. Heat half the olive oil in a small saucepan and sauté the chopped garlic and breadcrumbs over a very moderate heat for a couple of minutes. Pour the sautéed garlic and breadcrumbs into a bowl. Snip in the fresh herbs, and add a teaspoon of sugar, if liked. Stir until well mixed.

Using a teaspoon, fill the drained tomatoes with the herb mixture. Put a little knob of butter on the top of each filled tomato and season with freshly ground black pepper. Grease a suitable gratin dish with the rest of the oil. Cook in the bottom of the oven for 45 minutes–1 hour. Reduce the heat a little if the tomatoes look like collapsing. Serve warm.

Pommes de Terre à la Forestière
Sautéed Potatoes with Mushrooms and Bacon

This is not so much a recipe as a way of combining two dishes to make a substantial main course.

Chop 6 rashers of thick-cut rindless green streaky bacon. Turn to *pommes de terre sautées* on page 124. Add the chopped bacon to the rinsed diced potatoes and follow Madame Boucher's recipe, making sure you don't try to rush the process.

When the potatoes are halfway through the cooking, start preparing *champignons à la poêle*, using a sauté pan (see page 132). Gently combine the contents of the two pans and serve immediately with a large, sharply dressed green salad. Enough for 8.

LENTILLES AUX LARDONS
Lentils with Bacon

I LOVE LENTILS. The lentils that come from Le Puy, in the heart of the volcanic Auvergne region of central France, are the very best, and worth looking out for. The bacon in the dish below is a well-tried combination, but I sometimes omit it if I am in a vegetarian mood or serving the lentils as a side dish. Try them with roast chicken and, dare I say it, creamed potatoes (see page 123).

300 g/11 oz *lentilles du Puy* or small dark bluey-green lentils	Serves 4	1 tablespoon olive oil
1 medium-sized onion		30 g/1 oz/2 tablespoons butter
1 clove of garlic		a few sprigs of parsley and thyme
1 large ripe tomato		1 bay leaf
60 g/2 oz thick-cut rindless smoked back bacon		sea salt
		freshly ground black pepper

SOAK THE LENTILS WHILE YOU PREPARE THE other ingredients. Finely chop the onion and garlic. Blanch, seed and chop the tomato. Cut the bacon in half. Chop one half into small dice.

Drain and rinse the lentils. In a heavy-based large saucepan, heat half the olive oil and a knob of butter.

Add the chopped onion to the pan. Sauté over a moderate heat for a couple of minutes, then add the garlic and the lentils. Stir to mix with the onion and coat with the fat, then add the tomato and the unchopped half of bacon.

Add the herbs and the bay leaf, then pour in plenty of water to completely cover the ingredients, by at least 2.5 cm/1 in. Bring to the boil fairly slowly, then season lightly with salt and freshly ground black pepper. Cover, reduce the heat and cook for 25–30 minutes, until the lentils are soft but not mushy. Lift the lid every now and then to check the cooking and add a ladleful of extra water if necessary.

When the lentils are nearly cooked, heat the rest of the oil in a small frying-pan. Sauté the chopped bacon over a moderate heat until crisp and golden. Drain on absorbent paper. Drain the lentils of any excess liquid – reserve this for a soup, sauce or stock.

Discard the herbs and bay leaf. Slice the piece of bacon and return to the lentils. Swirl in the rest of the butter. Sprinkle in the sautéed bacon and serve immediately.

ENDIVES AU FOUR
Baked Chicory

Cʜɪᴄᴏʀʏ ɪꜱ ᴀ bit of an acquired taste. As children we certainly didn't rate it much. More often than not, we used to eat chicory plainly steamed, which we didn't at all like, sometimes pan-fried with butter, which was an improvement, and less frequently, baked as below. This was a real treat, especially when the chicory was wrapped in thin slices of ham before being returned to the oven for the final *gratin* stage. I now prefer this dish without ham, but then, I like the slightly bitter flavour of chicory a great deal more than I used to.

Serves 4

750 g/1¾ lbs chicory

60 g/2 oz/4 tablespoons butter

2 teaspoons sugar

sea salt

freshly ground black pepper

1 lemon wedge

3 tablespoons *crème fraîche* or double cream

30 g/1 oz Gruyère

Hᴇᴀᴛ ᴛʜᴇ ᴏᴠᴇɴ ᴛᴏ 180°C/350°F/GAS 4. Soften half the butter. Trim and rinse the chicory. Discard any bruised outer leaves. Spread the softened butter over a gratin dish just large enough to take the chicory in a single layer.

Arrange the chicory on the dish. Sprinkle with sugar, then season lightly with salt and freshly ground black pepper. Squeeze the wedge of lemon over the chicory. Dot with the rest of the butter and cover with foil. Bake in the oven for about 30 minutes.

Grate the Gruyère into a bowl and combine with the *crème fraîche*. Season with a little black pepper. Take the dish out of the oven. Turn up the heat to 200°C/400°F/Gas 6. Remove the foil, then spread the cream and cheese mixture over the chicory. Return the dish to the oven and bake for a further 10–15 minutes, until golden and sizzling. Serve hot.

PÊCHES AU VIN/*Peaches in White Wine*

POIRES AU VIN ROUGE/*Pears in Red Wine*

COMPOTE D'ABRICOTS ET DE FRAISES
Apricot and Strawberry Compote

CRÈME ANGLAISE/*Custard*

ŒUFS À LA NEIGE/*Eggs in the Snow*

ILE FLOTTANTE/*Floating Island*

GLACE DOUBLE À LA VANILLE ET AUX FRUITS ROUGES
Vanilla and Red Fruit Ice Cream

CERISES LÉGISLATIVES/*Cherry Ring*

GÂTEAU À L'ORANGE/*Orange Cake*

GÂTEAU GLACÉ AU MOKA
Iced Mocha Gâteau

TARTE AU CITRON/*Lemon Tart*

TATIN EXPRESS
Quick Upside-down Apple Tart

TARTE TATIN
Caramelised Upside-down Apple Tart

POMMES MERINGUÉES/*Meringue Apples*

MOUSSE AU CHOCOLAT
Chocolate Mousse

CHARLOTTE AUX AMANDES ET AUX PISTACHES
Almond and Pistachio Charlotte

PROFITEROLES AU CHOCOLAT
Chocolate Profiteroles

GÂTEAU AU CHOCOLAT
Chocolate Cake

GÂTEAU AUX NOIX/*Walnut Cake*

QUATRE-QUARTS/*French Pound Cake*

Desserts

Sweets and Puddings

When I was a child, puddings were a treat and I still think of them as such – something sweet and quite special to delight in when the occasion warrants.

My mother did not have a sweet tooth and she was concerned about *la ligne*, not so much hers which was most elegant, but that of her three daughters who were less streamlined. The result was that we seldom ate desserts at home, twice a week at the most. The national average is probably closer to once a day.

Instead we had cheese followed by fruit. We loved the former and dutifully munched the latter – to this day I much prefer eating fruit between meals, without knife and fork. Reading recently that it is healthier to ingest fruit on its own than during a meal made me feel righteous and vindicated.

Looking back on this absence of daily pudding, I am grateful for two reasons. The first is that I soon became a cheese lover, with a wealth of pleasures and interesting finds in store, not only in France but also increasingly in Britain. The second reason is that I was spared a lot of bad and filling sweet stodge. To my mind a boring dessert simply is not worth eating.

The French think of *pâtisserie* as an art. Like other families we relied on the best local master baker and bought in elaborate cakes and ices. What we did at home was the object of intense discussions and comparisons – after all this was no routine matter. Why did this *tarte Tatin* go wrong? Was not the *île flottante* particularly light? Perhaps there was too much orange flavouring in the chocolate cake ... All the recipes in the shortish repertoire that follows repeatedly passed the family test.

PÊCHES AU VIN
Peaches in White Wine

Pêches au vin, were a summer treat and a Fourchettes institution. In their crudest form, they were an unceremonious do-it-yourself-at-the-table concoction. While carrying on with the general conversation, you took an unpeeled peach, freshly plucked from the garden, chopped it up and tipped it into your wine glass. You then added a little wine – white, rosé or red, depending on what you were drinking at the time, and maybe a sprinkling of sugar. As children we made a happy sugary mush in our water glasses. We were already divided between drinkers and non-drinkers of wine, with some of us clamouring for a teaspoon of rosé, *pour faire comme les grands* – to do like the grown-ups. This was solemnly doled out by our grandfather. I don't think I need say which group I belonged to.

I can recommend the method outlined above, especially if you have a glut of bruised peaches. Steep them in lightly sugared wine and chill for an hour or so for a lovely casual dessert.

The recipe below is more formal and definitely more refined. You may like to compromise between the two.

	Serves 4	
4 white peaches		2 tablespoons blackberry liqueur, *cassis* or red fruit liqueur
300 ml/½ pint/1¼ cups white wine		
1 vanilla pod		8 almonds, shelled and blanched
3 tablespoons sugar		45 g/1½ oz shelled pistachios
3 tablespoons redcurrant jelly		a few mint leaves

PÊCHES BLANCHES
AU SIROP

PEEL THE PEACHES. PLUNGE THEM IN A saucepan of boiling water and keep bubbling for a couple of minutes. Lift out of the water with a slotted spoon – the peel should slip off easily. If not, boil a minute longer.

Meanwhile, prepare the syrup. In a saucepan large enough to take the peaches in a single layer, combine the wine with the same quantity of water. Slit the vanilla pod in half and add to the liquid. Stir in the sugar and bring to the boil, then reduce the heat and simmer until you have peeled the peaches.

Then add the peeled peaches to the simmering liquid and gently poach for 5 minutes, turning them over carefully halfway through.

Remove the peaches from the poaching liquid with a slotted spoon and leave them to cool a little.

Turn up the heat and boil the liquid until reduced by a good half. Stir in the redcurrant jelly and the blackberry or other liqueur. Carefully cut each peach in half. Remove the stone and place almonds in the cavities. Pour or spoon the syrup over the peaches.

Finely chop the shelled pistachios or, if you prefer, pound them using a pestle and mortar. Sprinkle the pistachios over the peaches. Leave to macerate until cold, then chill until needed. Arrange a mint leaf or two on top of each halved peach before serving.

POIRES AU VIN ROUGE
Pears in Red Wine

A LATE SUMMER and autumn dessert popular all over France. The prunes are a traditional Loire ingredient, sadly fast disappearing and much harder to find locally these days. For the addition of *crème de cassis* and the *brioche* suggestion I am indebted to a professional chef, my friend Ghislaine Salé of the *Auberge de la Brenne* in Neuillé Le Lierre, between Amboise and Châteaurenault. My original family recipe was somewhat more basic. Use handsome firm pears in peak condition for this recipe.

4 ripe but firm Williams pears	**Serves 4**	8 stoned prunes
600 ml/1 pint/2½ cups red wine		2 tablespoons *crème de cassis*
1–2 tablespoons sugar		little hot *brioches*, to serve, if liked
1 tablespoon grated nutmeg		

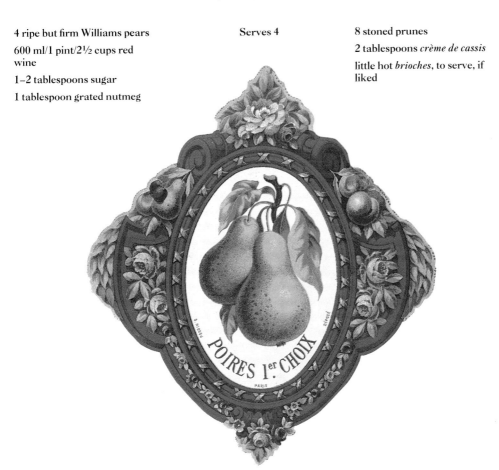

PEEL THE PEARS, KEEPING THEM WHOLE. IN a heavy-based saucepan large enough to take the pears comfortably in a single layer, combine the wine, sugar and nutmeg. Place the pears side by side in the liquid. Bring to a simmer. Add the prunes and simmer gently for about 15 minutes, until the pears are just cooked and tender.

Carefully turn the pears over once during cooking and baste occasionally with the simmering wine.

Using a slotted spoon, remove the pears and prunes from the liquid. Leave to cool on a serving dish or in individual coupes. The pears look best upright.

Turn up the heat, add the *crème de cassis* to the wine and boil until the liquid becomes a little syrupy and is reduced by a good half. Spoon or pour the syrup over the pears and prunes and serve *tiède* or chilled. If you are serving the pears *tièdes*, hot *brioches* make a splendid accompaniment.

COMPOTE D'ABRICOTS ET DE FRAISES
Apricot and Strawberry Compote

THE TRICK WITH compotes is not to allow the fruit to collapse into a purée. I like the combination below very much. It tastes even better if the raw strawberries you add at the end are *fraises des bois*, wild strawberries . . .

750 g/1½ lbs ripe but firm apricots	Serves 6	1 vanilla pod
150 g/5 oz/⅔ cup sugar		350 g/12 oz ripe strawberries
		½ lemon

IN A SAUCEPAN COMBINE 300 ML/½ PINT/1¼ CUPS water with the sugar. Split the vanilla pod and add to the liquid. Bring to the boil then simmer while you halve and stone the apricots. Add the halved apricots to the simmering liquid and continue to simmer for 8–10 minutes. Meanwhile, rinse the strawberries under cold running water, then hull them.

Remove the apricots from the pan with a slotted spoon and place in a bowl. Turn up the heat and bring the syrup to the boil. Reduce a little, then add half the strawberries to the syrup. Turn down the heat. Cook very gently for a few minutes. Remove the vanilla pod (dry and keep to use again), then add the poached strawberries and the syrup to the apricots. Stir, very gently, to mix.

Squeeze the lemon and, if they are very large, halve the rest of the strawberries. Add the strawberries to the compote, sprinkle with the lemon juice and very gently stir the lot. Refrigerate for at least 1 hour. Serve chilled.

CRÈME ANGLAISE
Custard

A GREAT ALL-ROUNDER that can be flavoured with a dash of strong black coffee, grated orange or lemon zest, liqueur or rum.
Crème anglaise is very flexible: the quantities below are average. For a thicker, sweeter cream, to serve, for instance, with a sharp fruit purée or compote, use less milk (450 ml/¾ pint/2 cups) and more sugar (120 g/4 oz/½ cup).

600 ml/1 pint/2½ cups milk	Serves 4	3 large or 4 medium-sized egg yolks
2 vanilla pods or a few drops of vanilla essence		90 g/3 oz/generous ⅓ cup castor sugar

IF YOU ARE USING VANILLA PODS, SPLIT them in half lengthways. Bring the milk to the boil with the vanilla flavouring. Turn off the heat and leave to cool. Meanwhile, in a separate saucepan, whisk together the egg yolks and sugar until smooth and pale.

Remove the vanilla pods, if using. Over a very low heat, pour the warm milk, a little at a time, into the egg yolk and sugar mixture, stirring well. Bring the mixture almost, but not quite, to boiling point very slowly, stirring constantly with a large wooden spoon. The cream will thicken gradually until its coats the back of the wooden spoon. Do not let it boil and take it off the heat occasionally while it is cooking.

Once the cream is cooked and thickened, strain it through a fine sieve or a *chinois*. If you are going to serve it cold, stir occasionally while it cools down.

Œufs à la Neige
Eggs in the Snow

This is a favourite party dish – light as a feather, festive-looking and, last but not least, economical. Another advantage of *œufs à la neige* is that they can be prepared a day or two ahead and will taste all the better for it.

Serves 4–6

900 ml/1½ pints/3¾ cups milk

300 g/11 oz/generous 1⅓ cups castor sugar

2 vanilla pods

5 large eggs

6 sugared almonds

FOR THE CARAMEL

90 g/3 oz/⅔ cup castor sugar

Bring the milk to the boil in a large saucepan with half the sugar and the split vanilla pods. Keep an eye on the milk while it is coming to the boil. Separate the eggs. Reserve the yolks. Whisk the whites until they begin to stiffen, then sprinkle in 2 tablespoons of sugar and whisk the mixture until very firm.

Lower the heat. Remove the vanilla pods from the milk, then scoop up 4 big spoonfuls of whisked egg white and poach them very gently in the simmering milk, for just over 1 minute each side, flipping them over carefully. Remove the egg 'meringues' from the milk, drain well, and reserve on a clean tea-cloth. Repeat the operation until you have used up all the whisked egg white, making sure the milk never gets back up to boiling point.

Strain the milk. In a saucepan, beat the reserved egg yolks with the rest of the sugar until smooth and much paler in colour. Turn the heat to very low. Pour the hot milk a little at a time into the egg-yolk mixture, stirring constantly with a wooden spoon, and cook very slowly until the cream begins to thicken. Never allow the mixture to boil, take the pan off the heat occasionally, and carry on stirring until the cream is just thick enough to coat the back of the wooden spoon. Remove from the heat and leave the cream to get cold, stirring it occasionally.

Pour the cooled cream into a large glass bowl and carefully arrange the cooked egg whites on top – they will float.

Prepare the caramel. In a medium-sized saucepan combine the sugar with 90 ml/3 fl oz /⅓ cup water, stirring until dissolved, then bring to the boil and continue boiling without stirring until you have a thick rich brown syrup. Immediately trickle this sticky caramel syrup over the egg whites.

Roughly crush the sugared almonds – I use a pestle and mortar or the small bowl of my food processor – and sprinkle them over the dish. Refrigerate overnight and serve very cold.

ILE FLOTTANTE
Floating Island

Another fluffy and hard to resist egg pudding that can be prepared well in advance. I believe that *île flottante* once described a layered cake of *brioche* or sponge, apricot marmalade, almonds and dried raisins set on a custard or red fruit purée, but I have never personally encountered the old-style pudding.

3 large or 4 medium-sized egg whites	**Serves 4–6**	To serve
120 g/4 oz/½ cup castor sugar	For the caramel	*Crème anglaise* (see page 140) or red fruit purée (see opposite)
9 sugared almonds or 2 small dry macaroons	**75 g/2½ oz/scant ⅓ cup castor or soft light brown sugar**	

Make the caramel. In a small saucepan combine the sugar with 5–6 tablespoons of water. Stir until dissolved over a gentle heat, then turn up the heat and boil without stirring until the syrup turns golden brown. Pour at once into a *moule à manqué*, ring mould or charlotte mould and swirl to coat all over.

Coarsely crush the sugared almonds or macaroons using a pestle and mortar. Heat the oven to 170°C/325°F/Gas 3. Whisk the egg whites until firm, then gradually mix in the sugar and crushed sugared almonds or macaroons. Continue whisking until the meringue mixture is stiff.

Bring a full kettle of water to the boil. Line the base of a large roasting tin with several layers of newspaper. Pour the meringue mixture into the prepared mould. Put the mould in the centre of the lined roasting tin. Pour in boiling water to come halfway up the sides of the mould. Cook the meringue in this *bain-marie* for about 40 minutes, keeping an eye on the level of the water. Pour in extra boiling water if necessary.

Leave the floating island to get cold before unmoulding it on to a serving dish. Serve chilled, over *crème anglaise* or red fruit purée. If using red fruit purée, stir into it the juice of a lemon and sweeten to taste with icing sugar instead of castor sugar.

GLACE DOUBLE À LA VANILLE ET AUX FRUITS ROUGES
Vanilla and Red Fruit Ice Cream

THIS IS A good ice cream for the berry season. Use the egg whites to make meringues.

600 g/1¼ lb mixture of some, or all, of the following: strawberries, raspberries, blackberries, redcurrants

150 g/5 oz/⅔ cup castor sugar

600 ml/1 pint/2½ cups double cream

Serves 8–10

strawberries and raspberries, to serve, if liked

FOR THE *CRÈME ANGLAISE*

350 ml/12 fl oz/1 ½ cups full-fat milk

3 vanilla pods or several drops of vanilla essence

4 medium-sized egg yolks

120 g/4 oz/½ cup castor sugar

MAKE A THICK *CRÈME ANGLAISE* (SEE page 140), strain it through a fine sieve or *chinois* and whisk it frequently while it gets cold. Rinse and clean the fruit. Purée in the food processor, then press the purée through a sieve into a bowl. Stir the sugar into the fruit purée until absorbed.

Whip the thick cream until firm. Reserve about one-third of the whipped cream and carefully fold the rest into the fruit purée. Pour or spoon the fruit and cream mixture into a tray and freeze.

Fold the reserved whipped cream into the cold custard. Flavour with a little extra vanilla essence if you like. Pour the mixture into a second tray of the same size as the first tray and freeze.

After about 30–40 minutes, remove both iced preparations from the freezer and stir to prevent ice crystals forming. Repeat the process twice, then leave until completely frozen – the vanilla ice cream is less likely to crystallise than the other.

Remove the trays from the freezer about 10 minutes before serving – the exact timing does depend on room temperature – and serve the vanilla ice cream on top of the red fruit ice in a serving dish. If you like, surround the ice cream sandwich with extra strawberries and raspberries.

CERISES LÉGISLATIVES
Cherry Ring

A JOLLY WAY TO enhance plain vanilla ice cream, bearing a joky title which, for the French, has republican or even revolutionary overtones. Rather perversely it makes me think of the poet Lamartine whose eloquence has to be thanked for the fact that the *tricolore* was not turned into a national red flag. As a man of Burgundy and a wine maker, he might perhaps have enjoyed the *crème de cassis* if not the sentiment . . .

	Serves 4–6	
450 g/1 lb sweet ripe cherries		2 tablespoons kirsch
40 g/1½ oz/2½ tablespoons unsalted butter	the juice of 1 large orange	2 tablespoons *crème de cassis*
4 tablespoons castor sugar	the juice of 1 large lemon	vanilla ice cream, to serve

RINSE THE CHERRIES AND REMOVE the stalks and stones. In a heavy-based saucepan, melt the butter over a low heat.

Add the stoned cherries, sugar, orange and lemon juice and simmer gently for 5–10 minutes, stirring delicately every now and then.

Drain the cherries over a bowl. Reserve the cherries and return the poaching juices to the pan. Bring to a simmer and reduce by about ⅓.

Add the kirsch and *crème de cassis*, then bring to the boil. Leave to bubble for 2–3 minutes.

Meanwhile arrange the cherries around piled up scoops of vanilla ice cream. If you are serving this dessert in individual coupes, allow 3 scoops per person.

Spoon over the sauce and serve immediately.

GÂTEAU À L'ORANGE
Orange Cake

ANOTHER RECIPE FROM MY aunt Yonnée, which makes me think of that old-fashioned institution, *le goûter de dames*, the ladies' tea, when the finest china came out and best behaviour was *de rigueur*.

	Serves 6	
125 g/5 oz/⅔ cup castor sugar		1 tablespoon Cointreau
90 g/3 oz/6 tablespoons soft unsalted butter, plus extra for greasing		FOR THE GLAZING
	1 scant teaspoon baking powder	5 tablespoons orange juice
2 large eggs		1 tablespoon Cointreau
125 g/5 oz/1 cup self-raising flour	1 large juicy orange	7–8 tablespoons icing sugar

HEAT THE OVEN TO 180°C/350°F/GAS 4. Beat together the sugar and butter until creamy. Beat the eggs into the mixture.

Sift the flour and baking powder over the mixture and fold them in lightly.

Grate the zest of the orange and squeeze out the juice. Stir the grated zest, the juice and the Cointreau into the mixture.

Generously butter a 1.2 l/2 pt/5 cup loaf tin. Spoon in the mixture. Knock the tin against the working surface to settle the contents.

Bake for about 50 minutes, until the cake is firm but bouncy to the touch and the blade of a knife inserted into it comes out clean.

Leave to cool in the tin for 10–15 minutes, then unmould the cake on to a dish.

Meanwhile, prepare the glazing. In a small saucepan, gently warm the orange juice and Cointreau. Stir in the icing sugar.

Using a pastry brush, paint the glaze over the cake – some of the glaze will seep in, the rest will form a light crust. Serve cold.

Gâteau Glacé au Moka
Iced Mocha Gâteau

Hard to resist. I tend to prefer this grown-up dessert without the optional extras, but candied angelica and glacé cherries make fine additions.

200 g/7 oz bitter chocolate	Serves 6–8	sea salt
2 tablespoons good quality instant coffee granules		90 ml/3 fl oz/⅓ cup brandy
		3 tablespoons kirsch
200 g/7 oz/generous ¾ cup castor sugar		about 27–30 *biscuits à la cuiller* or 36 sponge fingers
200 g/7 oz/14 tablespoons unsalted butter, plus extra for greasing		To serve (OPTIONAL)
		candied fruit
5 medium-sized eggs		glacé cherries

Break the chocolate into small pieces and place in a heavy-based saucepan with 125ml /4 fl oz/⅔ cup boiling water. Leave to stand for 3 minutes, then pour out the water and stir the chocolate over a very low heat until creamy.

Stir in the coffee granules, then set aside the pan over a bowl of boiling water, giving this cream an occasional stir.

Meanwhile, whisk together the sugar and butter until blond and foamy.

Separate the eggs one at a time, collecting the whites in a large bowl and whisking each yolk into the sugar and butter. Whisk the mixture well after adding each yolk.

When all the yolks have been incorporated, whisk in the chocolate and coffee cream, a little at a time. If it feels too thick and solid, beat in a tablespoon or two of hot water before adding to the butter, sugar and yolk mixture.

Add a pinch of salt to the egg whites and whisk until stiff. Now fold the whisked egg whites into the chocolate mixture, using a large metal spoon or balloon whisk, whichever you are most comfortable with. Start by folding in a couple of spoonfuls, then tip in the rest. The important thing is to work lightly and with upward movements to get air into the mixture. Stop working as soon as the egg whites are absorbed.

Generously butter a large 2.5 l/4½ pt/12½ cup loaf tin.

Combine the brandy and kirsch with 3 tablespoons water in a soup plate. Quickly dip each biscuit into this mixture and line the bottom of the loaf tin with a layer of biscuits. Repeat with a second layer of biscuits.

Spoon in the chocolate and coffee mousse. Knock the tin once or twice against the working surface to settle the contents. Cover with two layers of biscuits soaked in the brandy mixture.

Freeze overnight or for several hours, making sure the freezer is not turned to the highest/coldest setting.

Remove the iced gâteau from the freezer a few minutes before serving. Turn out on to a long platter.

If you like, arrange pieces of candied fruit around the gâteau.

TARTE AU CITRON
Lemon Tart

THIS IS MY version of my sister Françoise's recipe which she jotted down a long time ago at our cousin Florence's . . . It is sharp, zesty and a most pleasing way to round off a meal.

FOR THE PASTRY BASE

150 g/5 oz/10 tablespoons unsalted butter, plus extra for greasing

1 large egg

75 g/2½ oz/generous ¼ cup castor sugar

Serves 6

a small pinch of salt

250 g/9 oz/1¾ cups flour, plus extra for flouring

120 g/4 oz/8 tablespoons unsalted butter

200 g/7 oz/generous ¾ cup castor sugar

1 unwaxed orange

3 unwaxed juicy lemons

3 large or 5 medium-sized eggs

LEAVE THE BUTTER FOR THE PASTRY AND for the filling in a warm place until softened. Prepare the pastry base. In a bowl, whisk the egg with the sugar and a small pinch of salt until the mixture is light and foamy. Sift the flour into a second bowl, then tip it all at once into the egg and sugar mixture. Work the mixture lightly with your fingertips until it begins to feel like coarse sand.

Cut the softened butter into small pieces and work into the mixture until it is completely absorbed and the pastry smooth. Roll the pastry into a ball and refrigerate for at least 1 hour.

Heat the oven to 180°C/350°F/Gas 4. Dust a rolling pin with flour and generously grease a tart tin with butter. Roll out the pastry and line

the prepared tin – I invariably end up using my hands to flatten the pastry and fit it into the tin, as it is very short and breaks easily.

Now make the filling. Combine the softened butter with the sugar, beating vigorously until the mixture is smooth and even. Finely grate the orange and 1–2 lemons – the more zest you use, the sharper and more lemony the filling. Squeeze all the lemons. Whisk the eggs a little longer than you would for an omelette. Stir the grated zests and the lemon juice into the butter and sugar mixture. Whisk in the beaten eggs.

Pour the filling into the prepared pastry case and bake for about 35–40 minutes, until the filling is set and the base cooked. Cool before you remove the tart from the tin.

TATIN EXPRESS
Quick Upside-down Apple Tart

Nᴏᴛ ᴛʜᴇ ʀᴇᴀʟ thing, but very good indeed if you are pushed for time. The short-cut idea came from my cousin Isabelle who is a great believer in never spending more than a few minutes at a time in her kitchen.

Serves 6

750 g/1½ lbs crisp eating apples

60 g/2 oz/4 tablespoons soft unsalted butter, plus extra to finish

90 g/3 oz/generous ⅓ cup castor sugar, plus extra to finish

225 g/½ lb ready-made shortcrust pastry sheet

Hᴇᴀᴛ ᴛʜᴇ ᴏᴠᴇɴ ᴀɴᴅ ᴀ ʟᴀʀɢᴇ ʙᴀᴋɪɴɢ ᴛʀᴀʏ to 200°C/400°F/Gas 6. Very generously butter the base and sides of a loose-bottomed tart tin. Sprinkle liberally with sugar. Quarter and core the apples, then arrange them evenly and tightly in the prepared tin. Sprinkle the apples with the rest of the sugar and dot with the rest of the butter. Place the sheet of prepared pastry over the apples. Trim it to fit and tuck it in well all around between the apples and the sides of the tin.

Place the tin on the hot baking tray and bake for 20–25 minutes, until the pastry is cooked and golden. Check after 10–15 minutes and lower the heat if the pastry is browning too quickly.

Remove the tin from the oven and let it cool for a good 15 minutes. When it is cool enough to handle comfortably, cover the tin with a serving dish, then carefully turn both tin and dish upside down. Now remove the ring and base, easing them off the tart with a knife if necessary. Dot the tart with a little extra butter and sprinkle it with a little more sugar. Pop it under a hot grill until the butter and sugar bubble. Serve warm.

TARTE TATIN
Caramelised Upside-down Apple Tart

A WONDERFUL BUT tricky dish, with an infuriating tendency either to burn or not to caramelise enough. You can make a *Tatin* in a deep flameproof flan tin, but it helps enormously if you use the proper tin, a *moule à manqué*, which is round and about 5 cm/2 in deep. I have just invested in a heavy-based stainless steel mould which conveniently comes with its own serving dish. A good kitchen equipment shop should be able to supply you with a *moule à manqué*.

I would love to take part in a *Tatin* workshop – every cook who 'does' this dessert seems to have a different recipe. The method below is the one I am happiest with at the moment. I add 'at the moment' because it is likely to evolve: the sprinkling of sugar over the pastry is something I have only just started doing. To give credit where it is due, let me explain that it is a little *truc* my sister Anne-Sophie kindly let me on to the last time I congratulated her on the crispness of her *Tatin* pastry.

Serves 6–8

1.2 kg/2½ lbs crisp eating apples such as Cox's

120 g/4 oz/8 tablespoons soft unsalted butter

150 g/5 oz/⅔ cup castor sugar

FOR THE PASTRY

225 g/8 oz/1½ cups flour

1 tablespoon castor sugar, plus extra to sprinkle

1 small pinch of salt

150 g/5 oz/10 tablespoons soft unsalted butter

2 tablespoons *crème fraîche*

TO SERVE (OPTIONAL)

Calvados

crème fraîche

PREPARE THE PASTRY. SIFT THE FLOUR INTO a bowl, add the sugar and salt and stir to combine. Cut the butter into small pieces, then work it into the flour with your fingertips. Once the butter has been absorbed, work in the *crème fraîche*. Roll into a ball and chill for at least half an hour.

Melt half the butter in the tin – I do this on top of the stove, equipped with my thickest oven gloves. Remove from the heat. Sprinkle half the sugar over the melted butter and swirl to mix. Make sure that the edge of the tin is well coated with butter and sugar.

Peel and core the apples. Cut them in half, which is more traditional, or into chunky quarters, which I prefer. Arrange the prepared apples over the butter and sugar, packing them in tightly. Sprinkle them with the rest of the sugar and dot with the rest of the butter.

Place on top of the stove over a moderately high heat for 10–15 minutes, until the butter and sugar look golden and lightly caramelised. Keep a sharp watch on it to make sure the mixture does not turn too brown. Remove the tin from the heat, and leave until just cool

enough to handle. Heat the oven to 220°C/425°F/Gas 7.

Lightly dust a rolling pin with flour and roll out the pastry, not too thinly. Ensure that your circle of pastry is a good 5 cm/2 in larger than the tin. You may need to use your hands as well – this pastry tends to crumble easily. Carefully place the rolled out pastry over the apples. Using your fingers, tuck it in well between the apples and the edge of the tin. Sprinkle a little sugar over the surface to make it more crunchy and prick in several places with a fork. Bake in the oven for about 30 minutes, until the pastry is cooked and golden.

Remove from the oven. Leave to cool for a few minutes and cover with a serving dish slightly larger than the tin you have used. *Tarte Tatin* is best served barely warm. Turn over and unmould on to the dish just before serving, knocking the serving dish against the working surface and tapping the tin sharply.

Re-arrange the apples a little if necessary. Serve the *tarte* on its own, or sprinkled with Calvados and/or accompanied by a small bowl of *crème fraîche*, as you wish.

Pommes Meringuées
Meringue Apples

A GREAT HOMELY pudding that is easy to make and likely to delight the whole family, from the very young to the very old via most reasonably self-indulging adults. I am reminded of a celebrated *Tintin* slogan that really sums up the range of family enjoyment, – *pour tous les jeunes de 7 à 77 ans*, for all the young between the ages of 7 and 77. Does conscious enjoyment start at 7 and end at 77, I sometimes wonder? I know I liked Mado's meringue apples years before I reached the Age of Reason and my grandfather, who is turning 97 at the time I am writing, still much favours them.

For some reason, boring old ubiquitous French Golden Delicious apples taste better in France than they do in Britain. In this country I tend to use Cox's to make this pudding – the great sharp English Bramleys tend to collapse a little too readily.

This is not a difficult dessert to make, but do not rush it and allow plenty of cooling time between the various steps, in order to help the moisture to escape and the meringue to crisp.

The *crème pâtissière* – made with more milk than usual – is light and fairly thin.

750 g/1¾ lbs Golden Delicious or Cox's apples	Serves 6–8	1 vanilla pod, split, or a few drops of vanilla essence
butter for greasing		3 large egg yolks
7 tablespoons castor sugar	FOR THE *CRÈME PÂTISSIÈRE*	5 tablespoons castor sugar
3 large egg whites	750 ml/1¼ pints/3¼ cups milk	2 heaped tablespoons flour

MAKE THE *CRÈME PÂTISSIÈRE*. IN A saucepan bring the milk to the boil with the split vanilla pod or a few drops of vanilla essence. Turn off the heat and, if using a vanilla pod, allow the milk to steep for 10 minutes.

Meanwhile, whisk together in a largish bowl the egg yolks and sugar until the mixture is smooth and pale. Sift the flour into the egg and sugar mixture, then whisk again until well combined. Meanwhile, return the milk to the boil if necessary. Pour the boiling milk into the mixture and whisk until smooth and well-blended.

Pour the mixture back into the pan, and bring to the boil, stirring very frequently. Keep bubbling for at least 5 minutes, still stirring frequently, to give the flour plenty of time to cook. Leave the *crème pâtissière* to cool, giving it the occasional stir to stop a skin forming. Heat the oven to 180°C/350°F/Gas 4. Peel, quarter, core, then thickly slice the apples.

Butter a large ovenproof dish. Arrange the apple slices in the dish as evenly as possible. Sprinkle them with a tablespoon or so of sugar. Put the dish in the oven and cook the apples for about 15–20 minutes – they should be just tender but not disintegrating. Remove the dish from the oven and leave the apples to cool a little. Turn the oven down to 170°C/325°F/Gas 3. Pour or spoon the *crème pâtissière* over the cooled apples.

Whisk the egg whites until very firm, then gradually add the sugar, a little at a time, still whisking. Spoon carefully or pipe the beaten egg whites over the *crème pâtissière*. If necessary, use a fork or the handle of a spoon to make an attractive pattern. Leave a few very tiny gaps to allow any steam to escape from the *crème pâtissière* – this will help the meringue to crisp.

Return the dish to the oven and bake for at least 20 minutes, or until the meringue is golden and crisp. Serve hot or warm.

Mousse au Chocolat
Chocolate Mousse

Too many nasty concoctions go under the name of chocolate mousse – mean little messes of chocky *ersatz* and gluey gelatine, in small plastic tubs or large institutional bowls. To my mind chocolate mousse belongs in the home. All you need is good quality dark chocolate, eggs, unsalted butter, a little sugar and maybe a dash of spirits. You can then concoct a generous dessert that few will resist. A proper chocolate mousse should be deep brown, glossy and close-textured. Not a particle of gelatine in sight, just lashings of slightly bitter chocolate held together smoothly by the eggs and butter.

I like to flavour the chocolate with Cointreau, but whisky, rum or brandy also work well.

Serves 4–6

150 g/5 oz best dark chocolate	2 eggs	1–2 tablespoons castor sugar
60 g/2 oz/4 tablespoons soft unsalted butter	3 egg whites both at room temperature	a dash of Cointreau (optional)

Break the chocolate into small pieces. Grease a saucepan with a little of the butter, then melt the chocolate completely over a very low heat, stirring occasionally with a wooden spoon. Keep the heat very low throughout. As soon as the chocolate has melted, remove the pan from the heat and stir in the rest of the butter until it is completely melted.

Carefully break the eggs, putting the whites into a largish bowl and making sure they are entirely free of yolk. Gently stir the yolks into the chocolate mixture until they are thoroughly absorbed, then leave to cool. When the mixture is almost at room temperature, whisk the egg whites until thick and foamy. Add the sugar and carry on whisking until stiff and slightly glossy peaks form.

Using a large metal spoon or balloon whisk, fold a spoonful of whisked egg white into the chocolate mixture. Mix it in well. Stir in a dash of Cointreau, if liked. Then fold in the rest with the metal spoon or balloon whisk, whichever implement you are most comfortable with. The important thing is to work lightly and with upward movements to get as much air as possible into the mixture. Stop working as soon as the egg whites are completely absorbed.

Pour the mousse into a serving dish, stemmed glasses or ramekins and refrigerate overnight or for at least 3 hours.

CHARLOTTE AUX AMANDES ET AUX PISTACHES
Almond and Pistachio Charlotte

The fact that charlottes were probably a tribute to King George III's wife and could therefore be regarded as an English sweet, is largely forgotten in France where they are a popular family dessert. The word is used quite loosely, but charlottes tend to be a mousse, *bavaroise* or bombe mixture encased in biscuits soaked in liqueur or coffee and chilled in a deep rounded mould, wider at the top than at the bottom.

The recipe below impressed many a dinner-party guest at my parents' table, served on a fine white china-stemmed dish with a pale green and gold rim. I used to think that the green of the dish matching the pistachios was the height of refinement. With the considerable amount of kirsch absorbed by the biscuits, this is no nursery pudding but, on charlotte nights, we always stayed awake until we could hear that guests and parents were safely ensconced back in the sitting room. The nutty, boozy, exciting leftovers were then ours to feast on like sleepy vultures. This winner of a dessert is very conveniently made the day before the party.

About 20-24 *biscuits à la cuiller*, or about 30 sponge fingers

kirsch

225 g/8 oz/1 cup castor sugar, plus a little extra to sweeten the water

1 large egg

Serves 6–8

250 g/9 oz/18 tablespoons soft unsalted butter

250 g/9 oz/2 ¼ cups ground almonds

90 g/3 oz shelled pistachios, grated

Crème anglaise (see page 140), to serve

Soak the biscuits or sponge fingers in a mixture of kirsch and water sweetened with a little sugar. You will find the biscuits very absorbent, so do not use straight kirsch. Line the bottom of a 1 1/1¾ pint/4½ cup charlotte mould with biscuits, trimming them to shape, flat sides facing up. Then line the sides of the mould with slightly overlapping biscuits or sponge fingers, flat sides facing in.

Cream together the sugar, egg and butter until totally combined and smooth, then work in the ground almonds and half the grated pistachios. Flavour the mixture with kirsch and spoon it into the lined charlotte mould. Cover with soaked biscuits or sponge fingers. Top with a plate. Place a weight on the plate and chill overnight in the refrigerator. Keep the remaining pistachios wrapped in cling film in the refrigerator as well.

To serve, carefully unmould the charlotte on to a serving plate. Do not worry if some of the biscuits get a little damaged in the process. Pour over some cold *crème anglaise*, thus concealing minor disasters, and spoon more *crème* around the base of the charlotte. Sprinkle with the rest of the pistachios.

PROFITEROLES AU CHOCOLAT
Chocolate Profiteroles

MADO'S PROFITEROLES WERE absolutely top of the family pops, requested with amazing regularity for birthdays and other high days. *Crème pâtissière* is the more traditional filling, but we all loved vanilla ice cream. When I make this dessert these days, I use good quality bought-in ice cream rather than make my own. *Paresseuse* – you lazy girl, said Mado, the last time we discussed the dish on the phone.

FOR THE CHOUX	Serves 6	FOR THE CHOCOLATE SAUCE
120 g/4 oz/8 tablespoons unsalted butter		120 g/4 oz dark bitter chocolate
150 g/5 oz/1 cup flour		2 tablespoons castor sugar
250 ml/8 fl oz/1 cup water	FOR THE FILLING	2 tablespoons double cream
salt	Vanilla ice cream or thick *crème pâtissière*, made as on page 149, but using only 300 ml/½ pint/1¼ cups milk	30 g/1 oz/2 tablespoons unsalted butter
3 large or 4 medium-sized eggs		
dash of milk, for glazing		

CUT THE BUTTER INTO DICE. SIFT THE flour on a sheet of greaseproof paper. In a heavy-based saucepan, bring to the boil the water, diced butter and a very small pinch of salt. As soon as the liquid begins to boil, remove the pan from the heat. Quickly and all at once add the flour and immediately start stirring it in with a spatula or wooden spoon. Return to the heat and continue to stir briskly until the paste comes off the pan and looks smooth and a little shiny.

Remove from the heat and stir for 1 more minute. Add the eggs one at a time, mixing them in vigorously until the paste comes together again. Beat the last egg before you add it in, since you may need only a fraction of it: you should end up with a glossy, floppy paste, not a runny, liquid one. Continue beating for a couple of minutes to give the paste more body.

Heat the oven to 190°C/375°F/Gas 5. Grease a baking tray. Fit a piping bag with a plain 15 mm/½ in nozzle and spoon the paste into the bag. Pipe the paste on to the baking tray, shaping it into balls, about the size of a small tomato. Keep them well apart, at least 4 cm/1½ in. If you do not like using a piping bag, use a tablespoon instead – the end result will just look a little rougher. Brush the paste lightly with any remaining egg yolk mixed with a dash of milk.

Bake for about 30 minutes, until well risen and brown. Leave to stand 5 minutes in the oven before taking out to allow the choux to dry out a little. Slit the warm choux sideways almost but not quite in half, but wait until they are cold before you fill them.

If you are using *crème pâtissière*, you can fill the choux well ahead of serving. Spoon in a little *crème pâtissière* and keep in a cool place.

Prepare the chocolate sauce just before serving. Break the chocolate into small pieces. Place the pieces in a saucepan with 120 ml/4 fl oz/½ cup water and the sugar. Melt over a very low heat, stirring frequently with a wooden spoon. When the mixture is smooth, stir in the cream. Take the pan off the heat and swirl in the butter, stirring until it is melted, to give the sauce a nice gloss. If you are intending to fill the choux puffs with vanilla ice cream, do so after taking the chocolate sauce off the heat. Quickly spoon in the ice cream.

Pile the filled choux on a dish – they look much more attractive this way than in individual coupes. Pour over some of the chocolate sauce and serve the rest in a sauceboat.

LE GÂTEAU AU CHOCOLAT
Chocolate Cake

My idea of what a home-made chocolate cake should be – dark, rich, solid, irresistible and definitely for feast days. Over the years I have played with other ideas but I always loyally come back to this recipe. In my experience this cake disappears pretty quickly, but it will keep nicely moist for several days in the refrigerator wrapped loosely in foil. It also travels well, and will make you a popular weekend or party guest – but perhaps leave making the coating until you have arrived with your gift. The coating is over the top, and optional – but highly recommended.

200 g/7 oz good quality bitter chocolate

150 g/5 oz/⅔ cup castor sugar

175 g/6 oz/12 tablespoons soft unsalted butter, plus extra for greasing the tin

3 heaped tablespoons self-raising flour

Serves 8

5 medium-sized eggs

a small pinch of salt

grated zest of a small orange or a dash of Cointreau, to flavour, if liked

For the coating (optional)

200 g/7 oz good quality bitter chocolate

200 ml/7 fl oz/scant 1 cup single cream

4 walnuts, if liked

Break the chocolate into small pieces. In a large heavy-based saucepan, melt the chocolate pieces with 2 tablespoons of water over an extremely low heat, stirring frequently with a wooden spoon. Stir in the sugar and take the pan off the heat while you cut the butter.

Return to a very low heat and stir in the butter, a little at a time. Now sift in the flour, stir lightly to combine and cook for a couple of minutes, still over a low heat. Remove the pan from the heat and let the mixture cool a little.

Meanwhile, heat the oven to 170°C/325°F/ Gas 3, and generously butter a large loaf or cake tin, 2.5l/4½ pt.

Separate the eggs: the whites can be collected together in a large bowl but the yolks should be put on individual saucers – or an oyster place with its 'scoops' is helpful here. Work the yolks into the chocolate mixture, one by one, beating them in thoroughly. Add a pinch of salt to the egg whites and whisk until very firm and stiff.

Using a large metal spoon, fold the whisked egg whites into the chocolate mixture very thoroughly, but working lightly and with

upward movements. If you like, flavour with the grated zest of a small orange or a dash of Cointreau. Tip the mixture into the greased tin and knock the tin on the working surface a couple of times to ensure it is evenly settled.

Bake for about 45 minutes. Resist opening the oven door for the first 25 minutes, then check and turn the tin around if the cake is looking lop-sided. Turn up the heat to the next setting for the last 5 minutes – insert a knife into the cake to check that it is cooked: the blade should come out clean and dry. Leave to cool for a good 15 minutes, then carefully remove the cake from the tin and place it on a serving dish.

If you decide to coat the cake, wait until it is cold. Break the chocolate into small pieces and melt with the cream in a saucepan, over a very low heat, stirring frequently with a wooden spoon. Leave the mixture to cool a little, then pour it over the centre of the cake. Have a soft spatula at hand to smooth the coating evenly over the whole surface. Shell the walnuts and arrange over the cake, if desired.

GÂTEAU AUX NOIX
Walnut Cake

THE FRESHER THE walnut kernels, the better this cake will taste. It begs to be served with a cup of properly made coffee, but I once enjoyed it with a very vinous glass of mature Cahors.

250 g/9 oz fresh walnut kernels

3 medium-sized eggs

225 g/8 oz/1 cup castor sugar

60 g/2 oz/⅓ cup self-raising flour, plus extra for flouring

1 tablespoon rum

Serves 6

butter for greasing

FOR THE COATING

90 g/3 oz dark bitter chocolate

3 tablespoons single cream

30 g/1 oz/2 tablespoons unsalted butter

HEAT THE OVEN TO 180°C/350°F/GAS 4. Finely chop or pound the walnuts, reserving 9 attractive kernels. Separate the eggs. In a bowl whisk together the sugar and egg yolks until smooth and pale. Stir in the chopped walnuts, then sift in the flour and sprinkle in the rum. Whisk lightly to combine.

In a separate bowl whisk the egg whites until stiff, then delicately fold them into the mixture, using a large metal spoon. Work them in lightly, with upward movements, until absorbed.

Butter and flour a *moule à manqué* or deep flan tin. Pour the mixture into the prepared tin, knock the tin once or twice against the work surface to settle the contents, then bake for about 40 minutes until the cake is cooked and firm to the touch. Leave to cook for a few minutes, then turn out on to a rack and leave until cold.

To make the coating, break the chocolate into small pieces. In a small saucepan, combine the chocolate with 3 tablespoons of water and the cream. Heat slowly over a very low heat, stirring constantly with a wooden spoon, until the chocolate has melted and the mixture is smooth. Stir in the butter off the heat.

Pour the coating over the centre of the cake and spread it evenly with a soft spatula. Arrange the reserved walnut kernels at regular intervals around the cake, and place one in the centre.

Quatre-Quarts
French Pound Cake

Literally meaning four quarters – equal weights of egg, butter, sugar and flour – the French pound cake is a great stand-by, often served as a family dessert with stewed fruit *compote* (see page 140), fruit salad or, mid-afternoon, with a cup of tea (a more popular beverage in France than rumour would have it). Lemon, vanilla and orange are all traditional discreet flavourings. The ground almonds are a family addition.

2 large eggs or 3 medium-sized ones

150 g/5 oz/⅔ cup castor sugar

finely grated zest of 1 lemon or orange or a little vanilla essence

Serves 4–6

150 g/5 oz/10 tablespoons soft unsalted butter

150 g/5 oz/1 cup self-raising flour, plus extra for dusting

2 heaped tablespoons ground almonds

Heat the oven to 180°C/350°F/gas 4. Beat together the eggs, sugar, and flavouring until pale and a little frothy. Put the butter in a loaf tin or deep round *moule à manqué* tin and heat it in the oven until almost melted. Swirl to coat the tin lightly with butter, then pour the melted butter into the egg mixture a little at a time, whisking until thoroughly blended. Sift the flour over the egg and sugar mixture, a little at a time, then fold it in gently with a metal spoon. Now mix in the ground almonds.

Dust the tin with a little flour, pour in the cake mixture and bake in the oven for a good 30–35 minutes. If the top browns too quickly, cover it with a piece of foil. To check that the cake is cooked, insert a skewer – it should come out clean and dry.

Turn the cake out on to a rack as soon as it comes out of the oven and leave to get cold before serving.

The cake will keep well for a few days wrapped in foil and refrigerated.

INDEX

All recipe titles are listed in French and English.
Ingredients are indexed in English only.